Storytimes for Children

Storytimes for Children

Stephanie G. Bauman, Editor

LIBRARIES UNLIMITED

AN IMPRINT OF ABC-CLIO, LLC
Santa Barbara, California • Denver, Colorado • Oxford, England

Library of Congress Cataloging-in-Publication Data

Storytimes for children / Stephanie G. Bauman, editor.
    p. cm.
Includes bibliographical references and index.
ISBN 978–1–59884–565–5 (acid-free paper) — ISBN 978–1–59884–566–2 (ebook)
1. Storytelling—United States. 2. Children's libraries—Activity programs—United States. I. Bauman, Stephanie G.
Z718.3.S76   2011
027.62'51—dc22   2010033534

ISBN: 978–1–59884–565–5
EISBN: 978–1–59884–566–2

15 14 13 12 11   1 2 3 4 5

This book is also available on the World Wide Web as an eBook.
Visit www.abc-clio.com for details.

Libraries Unlimited
An Imprint of ABC-CLIO, LLC

ABC-CLIO, LLC
130 Cremona Drive, P.O. Box 1911
Santa Barbara, California 93116-1911

This book is printed on acid-free paper ∞

Manufactured in the United States of America

Owl and moon illustration by Stephanie G. Bauman

Contents

Introduction

Fast paced can seem like an understatement for today's busy librarian. Budget cuts, hiring freezes, more demands and fewer resources . . . sound familiar? In the midst of all this is a group of children who need you to prepare and conduct an amazing storytime program . . . and its tomorrow! But who has the time to create age-appropriate, interesting, fun, and educational storytime programs?

Library and information science graduate students, that is who! They bring a wide range of library experience, relevant learning, innovation, and of course a deep-seated need for good grades to the process of creating amazing storytime programs. In fact sometimes they are so good, they need to be shared. This book is a collection of just such storytime programs, created and collected by the graduate students of Professor Blanche Woolls at San Jose State University.

Each chapter of this book highlights a specific age group, customizing the programs to be relevant and entertaining to those children. Each grouping has several similar elements. The first is a distinct opening and closing, which can vary from a song to a train whistle or even a greeting/goodbye statement. It is important to have the same opening and closing routine for each of your storytimes, especially for younger children. This shows familiarity, sets the tone, and provides consistency. The body of each program varies according to age but always includes a literacy activity such as a book reading or two, booktalks, technology use, or reader's theatre. Also included in many of the programs, as allowed by time, are an activity, craft, or guest speaker related to the chosen theme.

At all times, efforts were made to honor copyright. Therefore, words to poems, rhymes, and song lyrics are included when they are in the public domain. For others, titles will identify the passage, and any paraphrasing of the wording will be given. Links and information pertinent to finding the titles will be provided.

It is my hope that this collection of storytimes is broad enough that it can be used in a pinch as well as for future programming. Suggested books can be substituted per your own resources or can be ordered new or used online, for those essential titles. This book should be a great addition to your own creativity, providing ideas and saving you some of that rare commodity: time.

Have fun, choose books that children will like! Remember to be silly, educate, create, and inspire!

1

Infants and Toddlers (0–2 Year Olds)

These storytimes are written for children who are 0–2 years old. The age group is great fun to have at storytime because the parent or caretaker is present, adding an additional and beneficial element. These programs enable parents to have a great interaction with their child through songs, rhyming, and finger plays. It is important to connect with the parents, especially if you want repeat visitors, so make it a point to know their names and conclude each storytime with additional resources and instructions for them.

This age group is sometimes known as lap-sit because the child sits on a parent's lap. This arrangement improves the level of interaction and can help keep the focus on the activities. The duration of each storytime is quite short, ranging from 15 to 25 minutes, to accommodate those short attention spans, and to avoid torturing the parents with too much baby talk and singing.

With this age group, storytime should include large picture books, bright colors, and easily recognizable items. The words are simple and usually rhyme. Infants and toddlers find themselves in a world awash with new sensations, so sights and sounds are very important. The activities recommended are usually interactive finger play songs, where the parent helps the child use their own hands to act out the words of the song. The child can then make connections between words and real-world objects (like their belly button) or just have a fun time moving to the music with their favorite person.

April Showers

Anticipated Length: 20 Minutes

Opening:

"Welcome to Rhyme Time! My name is Julie and I want to welcome you all to the library today. This week, we are thinking about April showers and we will be singing songs and sharing stories about rain. Your handout has all the words to the songs and a list of stories that we have in our library about spring. Please sing along with the songs and help your little ones participate as much as possible. We will have time to play together when our storytime is over. If your child becomes restless, please feel free to get up and move around the library and come back when you can. So let's get started!"

Opening Song:

Good Morning!
http://bussongs.com/songs/good_morning.php

Book Activity:
First Comes Spring by Anne Rockwell. ISBN# 0061074128
This is a lovely and short story with descriptions of spring themes, including flowers, rain, and birds.

Fingerplay Song:
(Parents help their child to act out the song's lyrics.)
Itsy Bitsy Spider
http://bussongs.com/songs/itsy_bitsy_spider.php

Song Activity:
Rain, Rain Go Away
http://bussongs.com/songs/rain_rain_go_away.php
(Repeat for all children in the group, or, if group is too large, just sing "all the children want to play.")

Book Activity:
The Mole Sisters and the Rainy Day by Roslyn Schwartz. ISBN# 1550376101

Song Activity:
Robin in the Rain
http://www.metrolyrics.com/robin-in-the-rain-lyrics-raffi.html

Closing to Parents:
I want to thank you all for coming today. Please feel free to stay and visit. Our books about spring are on the cart and there are extra copies of our song and story lists for you to take home. See you next week!

This storytime is based closely on a storytime written by Julie Andrews-Jotham.

 Notes

Babies

Anticipated Length: 20 Minutes

Opening:

"**G**ood Morning. I am very glad you all came. My name is Mrs. Turner. If at any time if your child is unhappy, please feel free to leave. Do not feel like you are a disruption. We want you to know the library is a happy place. Your child sees and experiences others babies in a much different way than they interact with adults, so today's theme is babies."

Opening Song:

Where Is (insert child's name here)? (To the tune of Where Is Thumkin?)
http://bussongs.com/songs/where_is_thumbkin.php
(Go to each child and play Peek-a-boo as you sing the song. You will need to sing the song several times depending on how many children are present. Encourage parents to sing and play along with their own child and the children sitting next to them.)

Book Activity:

Baby Face: A Book of Love for Baby by Cynthia Rylant. ISBN#1416949097
(I use the Elmo with a computer and LCD projector. I place the book under the Elmo and it projects the page on the screen. Parents can read along to their child.)

Fingerplay Song:

(Parents help their child to act out the song's lyrics with another child.)
Pat a Cake
http://bussongs.com/search.php?query=patty+cake

Book Activity:

My World Lap Edition by Margaret Wise Brown. ISBN# 0061667544

Activity:

Bubbles
(Have bubble solution and blow bubbles for the babies.)

Closing Song:

So Long, Farewell from the Sound of Music Soundtrack
http://www.stlyrics.com/lyrics/thesoundofmusic/solongfarewell.htm

Closing to Parents:

Parents, the library is open during posted hours, but we are open every Wednesday for your storytime. This will make it easy for you to come and check out books. Although

From *Storytimes for Children* by Stephanie G. Bauman. Santa Barbara, CA: Libraries Unlimited. Copyright © 2011.

you may check out two books at a time from the storytime table and keep them for one week, bringing them back the following Wednesday, you will find other books for parents in the children's room. Please take a few minutes to see what books we have that you can share at home with your child.

This storytime is based closely on a storytime written by Elizabeth Turner.

 Notes

Faces

Anticipated Length: 20 Minutes

Opening:
(Blow a train whistle to signal that it's time to start.)

"Hello everybody, my name is Josh. Thanks for coming to storytime. The theme for today is faces. Babies are first able to explore their world visually, and faces are the first and most common thing that they see and learn to recognize. Naturally faces are quite popular with babies, so let's begin with a song."

Opening Song:

Hello Babies (Tune of "London Bridge")
For this simple song you can make up your own fun lyrics.

> Hello Babies . . .
> How's your day?
> Let's go play!
> Say hooray!

Fingerplay Song:
(Parents help their child to act out the song's lyrics.)
Open, Shut Them
http://bussongs.com/songs/open_shut_them.php

Book Activity:
Baby Faces by Margaret Miller. ISBN# 0689819110

Fingerplay Song:
(Parents help their child to act out the song's lyrics.)
Face Play

> Knock at the door (Forehead Tap)
> Ring the bell, (A Little Tug at Each Ear)
> Lift the latch (Eye Lids Raised)
> Walk in (Open Mouth and Pop a Finger Inside)
> Take a chair (Touch Right Cheek)
> Sit down (Touch Left Cheek)
> Good morning, Sir! (Finger On Chin)

http://bussongs.com/songs/face_play.php

Book Activity:
Baby Talk (Flip-A-Face) by Harriet Ziefert. ISBN# 1593541058

Song Activity:
Baby Face from CD by same title created by kimbo educational:
http://kimboedcatalog.com/baby_face_cd-p-56165.html?osCsid=3f2bf06d851e63feb22f4d
cc664b8859
(Children and caregivers are encouraged to clap and sing along.)

Book Activity:
Big Smile, Baby! Illustrated by Charlotte Stowell and Photography by Phil Babb.
ISBN# 1407531417

Closing Song:
The More We Get Together
http://bussongs.com/songs/the_more_we_get_together.php
(Blow the train whistle to signal the end of storytime and the beginning of playtime.)

Closing to Parents:
Thank you all for coming to storytime today. I hope to see you again next week.
(Bring out toys for a 10-minute playtime session.)

This storytime is based closely on a storytime written by Joshua Mitchell.

Farm Animals

Anticipated Length: 20 Minutes

Opening:

"Good Morning. I am very glad you all came. My name is Mrs. Turner. If at any time if your child is unhappy, please feel free to leave. Do not feel like you are a disruption. We want you to know the library is a happy place. Today's theme is farm animals. They are a lot of fun for babies because images of them are everywhere, especially at the grocery story, and farm animals can often be visited locally."

Opening Song:

Where Is (insert child's name here)? (To the tune of Where Is Thumkin?)
http://bussongs.com/songs/where_is_thumbkin.php

(Go to each child and play Peek-a-boo as you sing the song. You will need to sing the song several times depending on how many children are present. Encourage parents to sing and play along with their own child and the children sitting next to them.)

Book Activity:

Twinkle, Twinkle: An Animal Lover's Mother Goose by Bobbie Fabian. ISBN# 0525459065

Fingerplay Song:

(Parents help their child to act out the song's lyrics.)
This Little Piggy Went to Market
http://bussongs.com/songs/this_little_piggie.php

Song Activity:

Old McDonald Had a Farm
http://bussongs.com/songs/old_macdonald.php

Book Activity:

Black on White: Who Are They? by Tana Hoban. ISBN#688129218

Song Activity:

Five Little Ducks
http://www.kididdles.com/lyrics/f005.html
http://bussongs.com/songs/five_little_ducks.php

Closing Song:

So Long, Farewell from the *Sound of Music* Soundtrack
http://www.stlyrics.com/lyrics/thesoundofmusic/solongfarewell.htm

From *Storytimes for Children* by Stephanie G. Bauman. Santa Barbara, CA: Libraries Unlimited. Copyright © 2011.

Closing to Parents:
Parents, the library is open only for parents, caregivers, and children for storytime every Wednesday for you to check out books for you and your child. Please take only two books from the storytime books. You may keep them for one week and bring them back the following Wednesday. Please take a few minutes to see what books we have that you can share at home with your child.

This storytime is based closely on a storytime written by Elizabeth Turner.

 Notes

Food

Anticipated Length: 20 Minutes

Opening:
(Blow a train whistle to signal that it's time to start.)

"Hello everybody, my name is Josh. Thanks for coming to storytime. The theme for today is Food. The world of taste can be both fun and scary, and babies are just starting to learn what kinds of foods they like, or they simply spit it out all over you! Today let's help babies get more curious about the world of food, and get started with a song."

Opening Song:

Hello Babies (Tune of "London Bridge")
For this simple song you can make up your own fun lyrics.

Like Hello Babies . . .
How's your day?
Let's go play!
Say hooray!

Fingerplay Song:
(Parents help their child to act out the song's lyrics.)
A Little Apple Seed (Tune of "Itsy, Bitsy Spider")

Once a little apple seed was planted in the ground
Down came the raindrops, falling all around.
Out came the big sun, bright as bright could be
And that little apple seed grew to be an apple tree!

http://www.preschooleducation.com/sapple.shtml

Book Activity:
My Very First Book of Food by Eric Carle. ISBN# 0399247475

Fingerplay Song:
(Parents help their child to act out the song's lyrics.)
Pat a Cake
http://bussongs.com/songs/patacake_patacake.php

Book Activity:
Let's Eat/Vamos a Comer by Alan Benjamin. ISBN#0671769278

Song Activity:
The Muffin Man
http://bussongs.com/songs/muffin_man.php

Book Activity:
All gone! By Ellio Kreloff. ISBN# 0934618127

Closing Song:
The More We Get Together
http://bussongs.com/songs/the_more_we_get_together.php

(Blow the train whistle to signal the end of storytime and the beginning of playtime.)

Closing to Parents:
Thank you all for coming to storytime today. I hope to see you again next week.
(Bring out toys for a 10-minute playtime session.)

This storytime is based closely on a storytime written by Joshua Mitchell.

Hands

Anticipated Length: 20 Minutes

Opening:

"Welcome to storytime everyone, my name is Stephanie. I am so happy to see everyone today! Today we will be participating in rhyming and fingerplay activities. Please help your child participate as much as you can. You can always leave and come back if your child needs a break."

Opening Rhyme:
(make action indicated by rhyme)

> When the sun lights up my room
> I wake right up and rub my eyes
> I get up for my breakfast time.
> I brush my teeth then comb my hair
> I put on clothes and lace my shoes
> I run straight away to story time
> To see my friends and make some rhymes.

Discussion:
You may have noticed your baby is experimenting with their sense of touch. As they explore their environment they are using their hands to feel for shapes, textures, and even temperatures. This is why books like *Pat the Bunny* by Dorothy Kunhardt are so much fun for them. Today we are going to help the baby create an awareness of their fingers through some fun songs and games that stimulate this tactile perception.

Fingerplay Song:
(Parents help their child to act out the song's lyrics.)
Where Are Baby's Fingers?
http://www.thebestkidsbooksite.com/fingerplays-for-kids.cfm

Activity:
Mirror
Turn your child to face you and take turns pointing to different parts of your face. This game is not so much for learning the actual names of those parts but experimenting with tactile sensation combined with the use of language. This helps your baby to associate touch with language. Use your own pointer finger to point to the part I call out, and then guide your baby's fingers to that same part on your face.

Fingerplay Song:
Ten Fingers
http://www.thebestkidsbooksite.com/fingerplays-for-kids.cfm

Closing Rhyme:
Wave Byebye to Storytime by Stephanie G. Bauman

> Storytime's over, but just for today
> So clap your hands and wave byebye
> See you very soon! Until next time!

Closing to Parents:
If you want more information or items to take home, I have put out a variety of board books about babies hands and tactile discovery on the back table. I will also be passing out a list of books such as *Ten Little Fingers* by Annie Kubler, that you can find at this library or if you fall in love with them, for purchase at local bookstores or online. See you next week!

This storytime was written by Stephanie G. Bauman.

Noises

Anticipated Length: 20 Minutes

Opening:

"Hello, my name is Jake. I'm glad you all could join us here today for the lap-sit storytime. Moms and Dads, please participate as much as you can. If your child gets restless or upset, feel free to get up and walk around for a few minutes. We want all their reading experiences to be positive ones."

Opening Song:

Hello Babies (Tune of "London Bridge")
For this simple song you can make up your own fun lyrics.

Hello Babies . . .
How's your day?
Let's go play!
Say hooray!

Book Activity:
Noisy Farm by DK Publishing. ISBN: 0756609879

Fingerplay Poem:
(Parents help their child to act out the song's lyrics.)
Tick Tock by Gareth Landcaster
http://www.fizzyfunnyfuzzy.com/showpoem.php?poemID=14

Book Activity:
My First Nursery Rhymes illustrated by Bruce Whatley. ISBN#069401205X

Fingerplay Song:
(Parents help their child to act out the song's lyrics.)
Barnyard Song (Tune: If you're happy and you know it)

If you're a chicken and you know it say "Cluck, cluck."
If you're a chicken and you know it say "Cluck, cluck."
If you're a chicken and you know it, then you really ought to show it,
If you're a chicken and you know it say "Cluck, cluck."
(repeat song with "pig, say oink, oink"; "cow, say moo, moo")

Book Activity:
Boom Boom, Beep Beep, Roar!: My Sounds Book by David Diehl. ISBN# 1600591140

From *Storytimes for Children* by Stephanie G. Bauman. Santa Barbara, CA: Libraries Unlimited. Copyright © 2011.

Closing Song:
The More We Get Together
http://bussongs.com/songs/the_more_we_get_together.php

Closing to Parents:
Thank you very much for coming. Please practice some of these rhymes with you children at home, I think they'll really enjoy it. The familiarity and repetition is good for them. We also have some board books in the back that are great for reading with babies. I hope to see you all again next week!

This storytime is based closely on a storytime written by Jake Sexton.

 Notes

Nursery Rhymes about Children

Anticipated Length: 20 Minutes

Opening:

"Welcome to Lap-sit Storytime. My name is Kathy and I'm so happy you are all here today. We are sharing rhymes, movement activities, and books. Please participate as much as you can, following along with the movements I make. If your child is not happy, feel free to leave and come back when your child is calmer. Today we are sharing nursery rhymes about children. Babies love the rhythm of these rhymes plus the sound of your voice saying them."

Opening Song:
(Parents help their child to act out the song's lyrics.)
Hey, Diddle, Diddle
http://bussongs.com/songs/hey_diddle_diddle.php

Book Activity:
(Parents help their child to act out the poems.)
Mary Engelbreit's Mother Goose: One Hundred Best-Loved Verses illustrated by Mary Engelbreit. ISBN#0060081716

Suggestions:

Wee Willie Winkie	(fingers running, stepping, rapping on palm)
Mary Had a Little Lamb	(use while lamb puppet to follow hand)
Jack Be Nimble	(hand over index finger pointing up)
Simple Simon	(put palm out flat, shrug with hands out)
Polly Put the Kettle On	(put curled hand on palm, take off, blow, hand over brow, blow, mimic drinking tea)
Diddle, Diddle, Dumpling, My Son John	(sleeping motion of head on hands, point to socks and feet)
Jack and Jill Went Up the Hill	(fingers climbing on upward slanted palm, hand on top of head, fingers rolling down palm twice)

Book Activity:
Little Miss Muffet by Tracey Campbell Pearson. ISBN# 0374308624
You can use a cute spider puppet to illustrate.

Closing Activity:
(Parents help their child to act out various body parts.)
Peek-a-Boo

Closing to Parents:
Please be sure to read nursery rhymes to your baby. Books of rhymes are here (point to the location near you) for your use at the library or to check out to read at home. This bin has board books for you to share at home with your baby. I have copies of today's storytime for you to take with you also. If you don't have a library card, we are happy to help you get one today. Please join us again next week.

This storytime is based closely on a storytime written by Kathy Burgener.

 Notes

Spring Critters

Anticipated Length: 20 Minutes

Opening:

"Welcome to Rhyme Time! My name is Julie and I want to welcome you all to the library today. This week, we are thinking about the critters we see in spring and we will be singing songs and sharing stories about them. These are animals that can be seen right from your baby's window! Your handout has all the words to the songs and a list of stories that we have in our library about spring. Please sing along with the songs and help your little ones participate as much as possible. Our program will help with early literacy skills. We will have time to play together when our storytime is over. If your child becomes restless, please feel free to get up and move around the library and come back when you can. So let's get started!"

Opening Song:

Good Morning!
http://bussongs.com/songs/good_morning.php

Book Activity:
Read to Your Bunny by Rosemary Wells. ISBN# 0439087171

Fingerplay Song:
(Parents help their child to act out the song's lyrics.)
Flutter, Flutter, Butterfly by Bonnie Woodard
(Use a butterfly puppet and fly around to each child.)
(Tune of "Twinkle Twinkle Little Star")
http://www.thebestkidsbooksite.com/supersongs.cfm?songsid=143

Fingerplay Song:
(Parents help their child to act out the song's lyrics.)
Two Little Blackbirds
http://www.songsforteaching.com/fingerplays/twolittleblackbirds.htm

Book Activity:
Bunnies: Three Minute Tales by Caroline Repchuk. ISBN# 0075291649
These are short and simple stories about bunnies. The large-format board book makes it easy for everyone to see.

Song Activity:
Robin in the Rain
http://www.metrolyrics.com/robin-in-the-rain-lyrics-raffi.html

Closing to Parents:
I want to thank you all for coming today. Please feel free to stay and visit. Our books about spring are on the cart and there are extra copies of our song and story lists for you to take home. See you next week!

This storytime is based closely on a storytime written by Julie Andrews-Jotham.

 Notes

Trains

Anticipated Length: 45 Minutes

Opening:

"Welcome to storytime. My name is Kathy and I'm so happy you are all here today. We will be sharing songs, rhymes, movement activities, books, and a craft. Please participate as much as you can, following along with the movements I make. Adults, if your child is not happy, feel free to leave and come back when your child is calmer."

Opening Song:

If You're Happy and You Know It
http://bussongs.com/songs/if_youre_happy_and_you_know_it.php

Discussion:
Today we are going to practice colors and counting by reading and looking at a book called *Red Train*. As we see each number, let's hold up the number of fingers to show it. (Place numbers on felt board using the colors shown in book for association.)

Book Activity:
Red Train by Will Grace. ISBN# 0439488362

Book Activity:
Chugga-Chugga Choo-Choo by Kevin Lewis. ISBN# 0786807601

Activity:
Train Rubber Stamp
Today I have a rubber stamp of a train engine. Who would like one on the back of their hand? (Use a washable ink pad.)

Book Activity:
Trains by Byron Barton. ISBN# 0690045301

Book Activity:
Freight Train by Donald Crews. ISBN# 0688129404

Activity:
Coloring train pictures with crayons and glitter pens.

Closing Song:
If You're Happy and You Know It

(Use the words "tap your toe" as the chorus)
http://bussongs.com/songs/if_youre_happy_and_you_know_it.php

Closing to Parents:
Please join us next week for another toddler storytime; remember to bring back the books you check out today. Books and additional resources about trains are on the back table.

This storytime is based closely on a storytime written by Kathy Burgener.

 Notes

Zoo Animals

Anticipated Length: 20 Minutes

Opening:

"Welcome to storytime everyone, my name is Stephanie. I am so happy to see everyone today! Today we will be participating in rhyming and fingerplay activities. Please help your child participate as much as you can. You can always leave and come back if your child needs a break. Today our theme is Zoo Animals. These animals are visually fun for children because they are active and often very striking (like zebras), and there is a local zoo in many areas."

Opening Rhyme:

Can't Wait For Storytime! by Stephanie G. Bauman
(make action indicated by rhyme)

I dream all night with stars above
But when the sun lights up my room
I jump right up and hug my dog
Before she races around the room.
Then mom calls my name for breakfast time.
I get all dressed up and feel so fine.
Then I brush my teeth and comb my hair.
All this fuss for storytime and I can't wait to get there!

Fingerplay Song:
(Parents help their child to act out the song's lyrics.)
Eeny, Meeny, Miney, Mo
http://www.thebestkidsbooksite.com/funfingerplay.cfm?fingerplayid=121
http://www.thebestkidsbooksite.com/fingerplays-for-kids.cfm

Fingerplay Song:
(Parents help their child to act out the song's lyrics.)
Animals
http://www.thebestkidsbooksite.com/funfingerplay.cfm?fingerplayid=180
http://www.thebestkidsbooksite.com/fingerplays-for-kids.cfm

Book Activity:
Zoo Animals (Baby Genius) by DK Publishing. ISBN# 0756602718

Fingerplay Song:
(Parents help their child to act out the song's lyrics.)
Five Little Monkeys at the Zoo (use a puppet)

>There was one little monkey at the zoo
>There was one little monkey at the zoo
>She was dancing all around,
>And she was crawling on the ground
>There was one little monkey at the zoo
>
>There were two little monkeys at the zoo
>There were two little monkeys at the zoo
>They were swinging from the trees
>And they were swatting at the flees
>There were two little monkey at the zoo
>
>There were three little monkeys at the zoo
>There were three little monkeys at the zoo
>They were jumping up and down
>And they were running all around
>There were three little monkeys at the zoo
>
>There were four little monkeys at the zoo
>There were four little monkeys at the zoo
>They were scritchin' and a scratchin'
>And on their heads they were a tappin'
>There were four little monkeys at the zoo
>
>There were five little monkeys at the zoo
>There were four little monkeys at the zoo
>They were spinning like a top
>And then they'd sit right down and stop
>Cause there were four little monkeys at the zoo

http://bussongs.com/songs/five_little_monkeys_at_the_zoo.php

Book Activity:
The Adventures of WonderBaby: From A to Z by Oliver Chin. ISBN# 159702001X

Fingerplay Song:
(Parents help their child to act out the song's lyrics.)
Elephant (use a puppet)
http://www.thebestkidsbooksite.com/funfingerplay.cfm?fingerplayid=76
http://www.thebestkidsbooksite.com/fingerplays-for-kids.cfm

Closing Rhyme:
Wave Byebye to Storytime by Stephanie G. Bauman

>Storytime's over, but only for today
>So clap your hands and wave byebye
>See you very soon! Until next time!

Closing to Parents:
If you want more information or items to take home about zoo animals, I have put out quite a few on the back table for everyone to look at. I will also be passing out a list of books such as *Zoo Animals* by Brian Wildsmith, that you can find at this library or if you fall in love with them, for purchase at local bookstores or online. See you next week!

This storytime was written by Stephanie G. Bauman.

 Notes

2

Pre-Schoolers (3–4 Year Olds)

Time to turn down the volume! These active pre-schoolers are high energy and excited about life. Bringing that energy level down just a notch is essential to finding a space where stories can be told and everyone can have some fun. That's why you'll find opening songs and activities in these programs that are active to the max. The pre-schoolers will find themselves skipping and waving and jumping to the tune of actions songs and verses. Then they will be ready to settle down and hear a good tale or two, or so you hope! For this age level, the stories have simple plots that are fun when acted out with silly voices and strange costumes. The children will want to see the beautiful illustrations so let them sit close. This is also a great age for puppet theatre, so be creative and let the good times roll!

Babies/Younger Siblings

Anticipated Length: 30 Minutes

Opening:

"Hello, my name is Jake. I'm glad you all could join us here today. Today we are going to be talking about younger siblings and babies that your toddler might meet. This can be rough for many children both from a jealousy aspect as well as learning how to be gentle with their play around younger children. Some of you have younger brothers and sisters who are babies, and are very small. All of you were babies not so long ago. And believe it or not, all of your mommies and daddies were babies once too!"

Opening Song:
Good Morning by Greg and Steve (We All Live Together Vol. 2 CD)

Discussion:
Today we're going to talk about babies.

Book Activity:
Ruby's Dinnertime by Paul and Emma Rogers. IBSN# 1841212865

Song Activity:
(Have children act out the song's lyrics.)
Shake My Sillies Out by Raffi (More Singable Songs CD)
http://www.metrolyrics.com/shake-my-sillies-out-lyrics-raffi.html

Book Activity:
What Should We Do With the Boo Hoo Baby? by Cressida Cowell and Ingrid Godon. ISBN# 1852692588

Poem Activity:
(Have children act out the poem words.)
Here's a Ball for Baby

> Here's a ball for baby
> Big and soft and Round
> Here is baby's hammer
> See how he can pound
> Here are baby's soldiers
> Standing in a row
> This is baby's music

Clapping clapping so.
Here's a big umbrella
To keep the baby dry
Here is baby's cradle
Rock, a baby bye.

http://www.odps.org/glossword/index.php?a=term&d=10&t=815

Poem Activity:
(Have children act out the poem words.)
Pat-a-Cake
http://bussongs.com/songs/patacake_patacake.php

Book Activity:
Babies on the Go by Linda Ashman and Jane Dyer. ISBN# 0152018948

Closing Song:
Goodbye by Francine Wheeler (Come Sit Beside Me CD)

Closing to Parents:
I have some books about babies on the table in the back of the room, feel free to take them home with you today. Or if you need help finding some other books that you think you'll enjoy, please come talk to me. I hope you've had a good time today, and that you'll come see us again next week.

This storytime is based closely on a storytime written by Jake Sexton.

Bears and Observing

Anticipated Length: 30 Minutes

Opening:

"Hi everyone, welcome to today's storytime! Thanks for coming. We are going to be doing a lot of jumping around, so don't stay too glued to your seat! Today we are going to be talking about bears! Let's get started!"

Opening Song:
(Have children act out the song's lyrics.)
Story Hour
http://www.thebestkidsbooksite.com/fingerplays-for-kids.cfm

Book Activity:
Where's My Teddy by Jez Alborough. ISBN#1406310964

Song Activity:
(Have children act out the song's lyrics.)
Bear Went Over the Mountain
(To the Tune of: "For He's a Jolly Good Fellow")
http://www.thebestkidsbooksite.com/fingerplays-for-kids.cfm

Activity:
You Are a Bear!
Students to pretend they are the bear from the song. . . .
What do you see on the mountain that is fun? What do you see in this room?

Book Activity:
Brown Bear, Brown Bear, What Do You See? by Bill Martin Jr., Illus. Eric Carle. ISBN# 0805087184

Closing Rhyme:
Storytime's Over
(Perform actions indicated)

> Raise your hands up,
> Give a Big Sigh,
> Storytime's over,
> Now wave Goodbye!

http://www.thebestkidsbooksite.com/fingerplays-for-kids.cfm

Closing to Parents:
I have laid out a variety of books on bears and also fun activity books for stimulating observational skills on the back table if you want more information or items to check out and take home. These types of books are look and see books. This is an important time to children to not only notice the world around them, but begin to make sense of what they see. They can do this through object recognition, direction, hide and seek, pattern seeking, and compare and contrast. An example of this can be found in the book *Hiding in the Woods: A Nature Trail Book* illustrated by Maurice Pledger. See you next week!

This storytime was written by Stephanie G. Bauman.

 Notes

Circles

Anticipated Length: 30 Minutes

Opening:

"Hello everyone. My name is Ashley. I am very glad that you came to join me at the library today. I would love lots of participation from both adults and little ones. We are going to begin by singing a great Hello song, so everyone join in and give a great big wave hello to one another."

Opening Song:

Hello Everybody
http://www.peterandellen.com/lyrics/helloeverybody.mp3
(Depending on the size of the group you can then repeat the song substituting each child's name for the word "everybody" in the song.)

Discussion:
Today we will be talking about a shape that goes around and around with no corners. (Trace a circle with your finger in the air.) Can anyone guess what shape that could be? That's right! Circles are everywhere.

Book Activity:
A Circle In The Sky by Zachary Wilson. ISBN# 053112570X

Activity:
Find Circles in the Room
Why don't we try and see how many circles we can find right here in this room. We can count them together.

Song Activity:
(Have children act out the song's lyrics.)
The Wheels on the Bus
http://bussongs.com/songs/wheels_on_the_bus_go_round_and_round.php

Activity:
Colorful Cars

1. Cut out basic car shapes from different colors of construction paper.
2. Cut wheels from black construction paper.
3. Have the children (with help) attach the wheels to the cars using split pins. The wheels can turn around and around like the wheels on a real car!

Closing Song:
Goodbye Everybody
http://www.peterandellen.com/lyrics/helloeverybody.mp3
(Same tune as Hello Everybody song, but you say Goodbye and See you Soon.)

Closing to Parents:
That was a lot of fun. I hope you all enjoyed talking about circles today. This is great time to learn about shapes. Take the time to point out the shapes that you see all around you every day. Have your child trace shapes on the pages of a book with their finger. I have set out some great shape books that you can borrow today if you like.

This storytime is based closely on a storytime written by Ashley Sealy.

 Notes

Colors

Anticipated Length: 30 Minutes

Opening:

"Good morning everyone. My name is Melissa and I am so glad to see all your smiling faces. Today we are going to be singing and reading stories, then at the end we will do a craft and your mommies can help you. I hope we all have lots of fun. Parents, you are more than welcome to sit behind your children on the rug if they need that added support to feel safe and comfortable, but if they will be okay on the rug without you, feel free to sit in the chairs along the side or back wall. If your child needs to go out for a moment, feel free to step out and rejoin us when you can."

Opening Song:
If You're Happy and You Know It

If you're happy and you know it clap your hands. (clap clap)
If you're happy and you know it clap your hands. (clap clap)
If you're happy and you know it then your face will surely show it.
If you're happy and you know it clap your hands. (clap clap)
If you're happy and you know it stomp your feet. (stomp stomp)
If you're happy and you know it stomp your feet. (stomp stomp)
If you're happy and you know it then your face will surely show it.
If you're happy and you know it stomp your feet. (stomp stomp)
If you're happy and you know it nod your head. (nod nod)
If you're happy and you know it nod your head. (nod nod)
If you're happy and you know it then your face will surely show it.
If you're happy and you know it nod your head. (nod nod)
If you're happy and you know it shout "Hooray!" (Hoo-Ray!)
If you're happy and you know it shout "Hooray!" (Hoo-Ray!)
If you're happy and you know it then your face will surely show it.
If you're happy and you know it shout "Hooray!" (Hoo-Ray!)
If you're happy and you know it do all four. (clap, stomp, nod, Hoo-Ray!)
If you're happy and you know it do all four. (clap, stomp, nod, Hoo-Ray!)
If you're happy and you know it then your face will surely show it.
If you're happy and you know it do all four. (clap, stomp, nod, Hoo-Ray!)

http://bussongs.com/songs/if_youre_happy_and_you_know_it.php

Discussion:
Today I would like to read some books about colors. Do you know your colors? What color is a duck? What color is the sky? What color is the grass? What color are clouds? Yeah, what color is your shirt? Great job everyone. Let's look at this book and see what

colors we can find in here. As I read this story, I need you all to help me know what the animals see.

Book Activity:
Brown Bear, Brown Bear, What Do You See? by Bill Martin Jr., Illus. Eric Carle. ISBN# 0805087184

Song Activity:
(Have children act out the song's lyrics.)
Pink

> My favorite color is pink, I think (shrug shoulders)
> But red is pretty too.
> It's one or the other
> Unless I discover (hold out one hand then other)
> I'm suddenly partial to blue!

http://www.thebestkidsbooksite.com/funfingerplay.cfm?fingerplayid=174
http://www.thebestkidsbooksite.com/fingerplays-for-kids.cfm

Book Activity:
A Color of His Own by Leo Lionni. ISBN# 0375836977

Song Activity:
(Have children act out the song's lyrics.)
Color

> Blue is the Lake, (point to the floor)
> Yellow is the sun, (point to the sky)
> Silver are the stars,
> When the day is done, (wiggle fingers in the air)
> Red is the apple, (make circle with hands)
> Green is the tree,(raise arms over head like branches)
> Brown is a chocolate chip cookie for you and me! (rub tummy)

http://www.thebestkidsbooksite.com/funfingerplay.cfm?fingerplayid=329
http://www.thebestkidsbooksite.com/fingerplays-for-kids.cfm

Activity:
Make a Rainbow
For our rainbows today, you will need a blank rainbow page, and then a stack of squares. You should have a square of red, orange, yellow, green, blue, purple, and violet. You are going to take each color and tear little pieces off, like this and glue the pieces on your rainbow, one color per row to make a pretty rainbow of colors. Here is my example so you all can look at it if you want to use it. Let me know if you need more paper to tear, we have a lot.

This storytime is based closely on a storytime written by Melissa Castagna.

Community Helpers

Anticipated Length: 30 Minutes

Opening:

"Hello everyone. My name is Ashley. I am very glad that you came to join me at the library today. We are going to begin by singing a great "Hello" song, so everyone join in and give a great big wave hello to one another. Today we are going to talk about the people who help us in our community. This is a great book about all of those people."

Opening Song:

Welcome, Welcome
http://wiki.kcls.org/tellmeastory/index.php/Welcome_Welcome_Everyone
(Tune of Twinkle, Twinkle Little Star)

Book Activity:

Jobs People Do by Christopher Maynard. ISBN#0789414929

Song Activity:
(Have children act out the song's lyrics.)
Community Helpers/ What do you do?
Recite each verse and have children take turns telling about each job and how doing it benefits others.

What Do You Do?
Teacher, Teacher,
What do you do?
I teach you reading
And writing, too.
Doctor, Doctor,
What do you do?
I help when you're sick
With a cold or the flu.
Counselor, Counselor,
What do you do?
I help you with problems
And I care about you.
Firefighter, Firefighter,
What do you do?
I help fight fires
That might hurt you.
Officer, Officer,

What do you do?
I help you stay safe
In all that you do.
Dentist, Dentist,
What do you do?
I clean your teeth
And keep your gums healthy, too.
Children, Children,
What will you do?
When you grow up,
Which job is for you?

http://www.hummingbirded.com/community-helpers.html

Book Activity:
Community Helpers from A to Z by Bobbie Kalman. ISBN#086505374X

Song Activity:
(Have children act out the song's lyrics.)
The People in Your Neighborhood
http://www.lyricsdownload.com/muppets-the-people-in-your-neighborhood-lyrics.html

Closing Song:
The End from Early literacy storytimes @ your library: partnering with caregivers for success by Saroj Nadkarni Ghoting and Pamela Martin-Díaz (Tune of Twinkle Twinkle Little Star)
http://is.gd/5hf7M

This storytime is based closely on a storytime written by Ashley Sealy.

Dogs and Directions

Anticipated Length: 40 Minutes

Opening:

"Hi everyone, welcome to today's storytime! Thanks for coming. We are going to be doing a lot of jumping around, so don't stay too glued to your seat! Today we are going to be talking about dogs! Let's get started!"

Opening Song:
(Have children act out the song's lyrics.)

Story Hour

http://www.thebestkidsbooksite.com/fingerplays-for-kids.cfm

Song Activity:
(Have children act out the song's lyrics.)
Poodle in a Puddle
From *Move over Mother Goose* by Ruth McDowell. ISBN# 9780876591130

Book Activity:
Don't Lick the Dog: Making Friends with Dogs by Wendy Wahman.
ISBN# 0805087338

Song Activity:
(Have children act out the song's lyrics.)
Hungry Flea
From *Move over Mother Goose* by Ruth McDowell. ISBN# 9780876591130

Book Activity:
Bad Dog, Marley! by John Grogan and Richard Cowdrey. ISBN# 006117114X

Song Activity:
(Have children act out the song's lyrics.)
Point to the Right

Point to the right of me.
Point to the left of me.
Point up above me.

Point down below.
Right, left, up.
And down so slow.

http://bussongs.com/songs/point_to_the_right.php

Closing Rhyme:
Storytime's Over
(Perform actions indicated)

Raise your hands up,
Give a Big Sigh,
Storytime's over,
Now wave Goodbye!

http://www.thebestkidsbooksite.com/fingerplays-for-kids.cfm

Closing to Parents:
If you want more information or items to take home, you will find all sorts of books on dogs and learning directions on the back table. Dogs are constantly getting direction from their owners about where they should be, so what a great opportunity to help your child learn their directions in a positive way! Have them teach a pet stuffed animal dog at home how to walk in all the directions. See you next week!

This storytime was written by Stephanie G. Bauman.

Dinosaurs and Colors

Anticipated Length: 40 Minutes

Opening:

"Hi everyone, welcome to today's Storytime! Thanks for coming. We are going to be doing a lot of jumping around, so don't stay too glued to your seat! Today we are going to be talking about dinosaurs and learning about colors. Let's get started!"

Opening Song:
(Have children act out the song's lyrics.)
Story Hour
http://www.thebestkidsbooksite.com/fingerplays-for-kids.cfm

Song Activity:
(Have children act out the song's lyrics.)
Dinosaur's were

Dinosaurs lived long ago.
Some walked (stomp in place)
Some swam (pretend to swim)
Some flew, you know! (flap arms at sides)
Some were big (hold hands high)
Some were small (hold hands low)
Some were gigantic (stretch arms out wide)
V-e-r-y tall! (stretch arms up high)

http://www.thebestkidsbooksite.com/fingerplays-for-kids.cfm

Book Activity:
How Do Dinosaurs Learn Their Colors by Jane Yolen and Mark Teague.
ISBN# 0439856531

Song Activity:
(Have children act out the song's lyrics.)
Colors
(Sing the song to the tune of "Skip to My Lou") From:
101 Rhythm Instrument Activities for Young Children by A. Connors.
ISBN# 9780876592908

Activity:
Coloring Dinosaurs!
Crayons and premade simple stencils of dino's are all that's needed.

Closing Rhyme:
Wave byebye to Storytime by Stephanie G. Bauman

> Storytime's over, but only for today
> So clap your hands and wave byebye
> See you very soon! Until next time!

Closing to Parents:
This is a great time for your child to put the names of colors to objects all over their world! You will find books on dinosaurs and learning colors on the back table if you want more information or items to check out to take home.

This storytime was written by Stephanie G. Bauman.

 Notes

Ducks and Counting

Anticipated Length: 40 Minutes

Opening:

"Hi everyone, welcome to today's storytime! Thanks for coming. We are going to be doing a lot of jumping around, so don't stay too glued to your seat! Today we are going to be talking about ducks and baby ducks, called ducklings, and even learning about numbers. Let's get started!"

Opening Song:
(Have children act out the song's lyrics.)
Story Hour
http://www.thebestkidsbooksite.com/fingerplays-for-kids.cfm

Song Activity:
(Have children act out the song's lyrics.)
Little Ducklings
http://www.thebestkidsbooksite.com/fingerplays-for-kids.cfm

Book Activity:
10 Little Rubber Ducks by Eric Carle. ISBN#0060740752

Song Activity:
(Have children act out the song's lyrics.)
Counting Ducks from fingerplays and action verses for children by D. Labensohn.
http://www.nncc.org/Curriculum/fingerplay.html

Book Activity:
Nine Ducks Nine by Sarah Hayes. ISBN# 0763638161

Activity:
Duck, Duck, Goose (Especially for an older crowd of children.)

Closing Rhyme:
Storytime's Over
(Perform actions indicated)

> Raise your hands up,
> Give a Big Sigh,
> Storytime's over,
> Now wave Goodbye!

http://www.thebestkidsbooksite.com/fingerplays-for-kids.cfm

Closing to Parents:
All sorts of books on counting and ducks and baby birds are on the back table if you want more information or items to check out to take home. This is an ideal time to start learning simple numbers and counting. Give your children a reason to learn to count, let them help you with small tasks, like counting each button you are doing up on your jacket!

This storytime was written by Stephanie G. Bauman.

 Notes

Family

Anticipated Length: 45 Min

Opening:

"Good afternoon everyone. I am so glad you all came. My name is Mrs. Turner. Are you ready to read some stories and have some fun? Okay. Show me my good listeners. Good listeners are sitting criss-cross applesauce, hands in your lap. (Demonstrate how you expect them to sit.)"

Opening Song:

Open, Shut Them
http://bussongs.com/songs/open_shut_them.php

Book Activity:
What Dads Can't Do by Douglas Wood. ISBN#0689826206

Song Activity:
(Have children act out the song's lyrics.)
My Family
http://www.thebestkidsbooksite.com/funfingerplay.cfm?fingerplayid=77
http://www.thebestkidsbooksite.com/fingerplays-for-kids.cfm

Focus Activity:
If You Can Hear Me, Touch your _____.

Book Activity:
What Moms Can't Do by Douglas Wood. ISBN# 068983358X

Song Activity:
(Have children act out the song's lyrics.)
This Old Man
http://www.kididdles.com/lyrics/t032.html

Activity:
Make a card for a parent
See instructions:
http://www.dltk-holidays.com/mom/mmuffin-mom.htm
http://www.dltk-holidays.com/dad/necktie_craft.htm

Closing Song:
Dwarf Chorus. *Heigh Ho.* From the Disney Snow White Movie Sound Track.
http://www.stlyrics.com/songs/s/snowwhiteandthesevendwarfs21817/heighho564894
.html

Closing to Parents:
Boys and girls, I need to talk to your parents for just a minute, but you need to listen too, because grown-ups forget things sometimes and you can help them remember. Parents, be sure and visit the children's area and check out some books to take home and share with your child.

This storytime is based closely on a storytime written by Elizabeth Turner.

 Notes

Five Senses

Anticipated Length: 30 Minutes

Opening:

"Good morning everyone. My name is Melissa and I am so glad to see all your smiling faces. Today we are going to be singing and listening to stories. Then at the end we will do a craft and your mommies or daddies can help you. I hope we all have lots of fun. Parents, you are more than welcome to sit behind your children on the rug if they need that added support to feel safe and comfortable, but if they will be okay on the rug without you, feel free to sit in the chairs along the side or back wall. If your child needs to go out for a moment, feel free to step out and rejoin us when you can."

Opening Song:

If You're Happy and You Know It
http://bussongs.com/songs/if_youre_happy_and_you_know_it.php

Discussion:
Today I would like to share some books about our senses: seeing, hearing, smelling, touching, and tasting. It is fun to learn what our bodies can do and to learn about different ways we experience the world. I am going to start with a book activity.

Book Activity:
Your Senses by Helen Frost. ISBN# 073684869X

Book Activity:
Hello Ocean by Pam Munoz Ryan. ISBN# 0881069884

Song Activity:
(Have children act out the song's lyrics.)
Two Little Eyes
http://www.thebestkidsbooksite.com/funfingerplay.cfm?fingerplayid=18
http://www.thebestkidsbooksite.com/fingerplays-for-kids.cfm

Book Activity:
Panda Bear, Panda Bear, What Do You See? by Bill Martin Jr., Illus. Eric Carle. ISBN# 080508102X

Book Activity:
Polar Bear, Polar Bear, What Do You Hear? by Bill Martin Jr., Illus. Eric Carle. ISBN# 0805053883

Song Activity:
(Have children act out the song's lyrics.)
I Have a Nose

> On my face, I have a nose (touch nose)
> And way down here I have ten toes (touch toes)
> I have two eyes that I can blink (point to eyes)
> I have a head to help me think (point to head)
> I have a chin and very near (point to chin)
> I have two ears so I can hear (point to ears)
> Here are my arms to hold up high (raise arms)
> And here is my hand to wave good-bye (wave)

http://www.thebestkidsbooksite.com/fingerplays-for-kids.cfm

Activity:
Five Sense's Craft
Children color a picture then glue items on to represent each sense. (Use items such as scratch and sniff stickers, sand paper, candy wrappers, and so on.)

Closing Song:
The More We Get Together
http://bussongs.com/songs/the_more_we_get_together.php

This storytime is based closely on a storytime written by Melissa Castagna.

Food

Anticipated Length: 30 Minutes

Opening:
(Blow a train whistle to signal that it's time to start.)

"Hello everybody, my name is Josh. Thanks for coming to storytime. Today, we are going to be talking about food. Let's start with a song."

Opening Song:
Hands Go Up and Down (Opening Version) (Sung to: "Twinkle Twinkle Little Star")

> Hands go up and hands go down,
> I can turn around and round.
> I can jump upon two shoes.
> I can listen; so can you.
> I can sit.
> I'll show you how.
> Storytime is starting now.

http://www.carmel.lib.in.us/child/view.cfm?idnum=158
http://ysostorytime.pbworks.com/Storytime-Openings-and-Closings

Book Activity:
The Very Hungry Caterpillar by Eric Carle. ISBN# 0399247459

Song Activity:
(Have children act out the song's lyrics.)
Five Fat Peas

> Five fat peas in a pea pod pressed (children hold hand in a fist)
> One grew, two grew, so did all the rest. (put thumb and fingers up one by one)
> They grew and grew (raise hand in the air very slowly)
> And did not stop,
> Until one day
> The pod went POP! (Have children clap hands together.)

http://bussongs.com/songs/five_fat_peas.php

Book Activity:
Pete's a Pizza by William Steig. ISBN# 0062051571

Song Activity:
(Have children act out the song's lyrics.)
The Muffin Man
http://bussongs.com/songs/muffin_man.php

Book Activity:
Peanut Butter and Jelly: A Play Rhyme by Nadine Bernard Westcott.
ISBN# 0525443177

Closing Song:
Hands Go Up and Down (Closing Version)

> Hands go up and hands go down.
> I can turn round and round.
> I can jump upon two shoes.
> I can clap and so can you!
> I can wave,
> I'll show you how.
> Storytime is done for now.

http://ysostorytime.pbworks.com/Storytime-Openings-and-Closings
(See the last song at the bottom of the screen for correct version.)

(Blow the train whistle to signal the end of storytime and the beginning of playtime.)

Closing to Parents:
Thank you all for coming to storytime today. I hope to see you again next week!
Parents, I have left books and resources on food and nutrition on the back table.

This storytime is based closely on a storytime written by Joshua Mitchell.

Insects

Anticipated Length: 45 Minutes

Opening:

"**W**elcome to storytime. My name is Kathy and I'm so happy you are all here today. We will be sharing songs, rhymes, movement activities, books, and a craft. Please participate as much as you can, following along with the movements I make. Adults, if your child is not happy, feel free to leave and come back when your child is calmer."

Opening Song:

If You're Happy and You Know It
http://bussongs.com/songs/if_youre_happy_and_you_know_it.php

Discussion:
Today we are going to practice colors and counting by reading and looking at "How Many Bugs in a Box?" Before we lift the flap on the box help me know what color the box is by saying it out loud. As we see each number, let's hold up the number of fingers to show it. (Place numbers on felt board for association.)

Book Activity:
How Many Bugs in a Box? by David A. Carter. ISBN# 1416908048

Book Activity:
Molly in the Garden by Kate Pope and Liz Pope. ISBN# 0764161083

Activity:
Butterfly Stamp
Today I have a rubber stamp of a butterfly. Who would like one on the back of their hand? (Use a washable ink pad.)

Book Activity:
In the Garden: Who's Been Here? by Lindsay Barrett George. ISBN# 0060787627

Activity:
Craft
Today we are going to make insect cards using folded in half cardstock paper and insect stickers. You will be able to use whatever insects you like and draw other designs with crayons.

Closing Song:

If You're Happy and You Know It

(Use the words "tap your toe" as the chorus.)

http://bussongs.com/songs/if_youre_happy_and_you_know_it.php

Closing to Parents:

Please join us next week for another toddler storytime; remember to bring back the books you check out today. You will be able to take different books next week.

This storytime is based closely on a storytime written by Kathy Burgener.

 Notes

Kitties

Anticipated Length: 30 Minutes

Opening:
(Blow a train whistle to signal that it's time to start.)

"Hello everybody, my name is Josh. Thanks for coming to storytime. Today we are going to be taking about kitties. Let's start with a song."

Opening Song:
Hands Go Up and Down (Opening Version) (Sung to: "Twinkle Twinkle Little Star")

> Hands go up and hands go down,
> I can turn around and round.
> I can jump upon two shoes.
> I can listen; so can you.
> I can sit.
> I'll show you how.
> Storytime is starting now.

http://www.carmel.lib.in.us/child/view.cfm?idnum=158

http://ysostorytime.pbworks.com/Storytime-Openings-and-Closings

Book Activity:
Have You Seen My Cat? by Eric Carle. ISBN# 0887080545

Song Activity:
(Have children act out the song's lyrics.)
Five Little Kittens
http://childrenonlyeslefl.com/membercategorypages/songpages/animalsongs
chants1.asp
http://stepbystepcc.com/animals/cats.html

Book Activity:
Have You Got My Purr? *by Judy West. ISBN# 0525463909*

Song Activity:
(Have children act out the song's lyrics.)
The Mouse Ran Around The Room
(To the tune of "The Bear Went Over the Mountain")
Source: http://stepbystepcc.com/animals/cats.html

Book Activity:
Cat and Mouse in the Snow by Tomasz Bogacki. ISBN# 0374311927

Closing Song:
Hands Go Up and Down (Closing Version)

> Hands go up and hands go down.
> I can turn round and round.
> I can jump upon two shoes.
> I can clap and so can you!
> I can wave,
> I'll show you how.
> Storytime is done for now.

http://ysostorytime.pbworks.com/Storytime-Openings-and-Closings
(See the last song at the bottom of the screen for the correct version.)

(Blow the train whistle to signal the end of storytime and the beginning of playtime.)

Closing to Parents:
Thank you all for coming to storytime today. I hope to see you again next week!
Parents, I have left books and resources on cats and having pets on the back table.

This storytime is based closely on a storytime written by Joshua Mitchell.

Mo Willems Knuffle Bunny

Anticipated Length: 45 Minutes

Opening:

"**G**ood morning boys and girls. I am so glad that you came today. We are going to have lots of fun today, reading together, singing songs, playing games, and doing crafts. Sometimes you will get to play and sometimes you will have to be quiet and listen. When I stand up, you can play but when I sit you have to be quiet and listen. Let's practice. (Stand up and tell them to stand up and wiggle. Sit down and have them all sit down. But make it a game. Praise those that catch on.) Parents if at any time your child does not want to participate feel free to take them out and bring them back whenever they are ready. Okay, let's all stand up and sing our first song."

Opening Song:

If You're Happy and You Know It
http://www.kididdles.com/lyrics/i007.html

(My last verse is a quiet last verse.)
If you're happy and you know it, sit like this. (Model the way you want them to sit for the story.)

Discussion:

Boys and girls does anyone have something special that they just can't live without, like a blankie, or a teddy bear? I do. That's right, I'm a grown up and I have a pillow I take with me whenever I go to spend the night somewhere else. I can't sleep without my pillow. I can sleep on the floor if I have my pillow, but I can't sleep anywhere without my pillow. The girl in our story today has a special friend that she takes with her everywhere. Let's read about it. Where are my good listeners?

Book Activity:
Knuffle Bunny: A Cautionary Tale by Mo Willems. ISBN#0786818700

Song Activity:
(Have children act out the song's lyrics.)
Head and Shoulders, Knees and Toes
http://www.kididdles.com/lyrics/h002.html
(Only instead of just pointing to their ears, children make bunny ears with their fingers to pretend they are Knuffle Bunny.)

Book Activity:
Knuffle Bunny: A Case of Mistaken Identity by Mo Willems. ISBN#1423102991

Song Activity:
(Have children act out the song's lyrics.)
Little Rabbit
http://www.thebestkidsbooksite.com/funfingerplay.cfm?fingerplayid=500
http://www.thebestkidsbooksite.com/fingerplays-for-kids.cfm

Activity:
Stick the Tail on the Bunny
Create a bunny coloring handout with a glued on cotton tail.

Closing Song:
Time to Say Goodbye by Jean Warren
http://www.preschoolexpress.com/music_station03/music_station_may03.shtml
(Tune: "Up on the House Top")

This storytime is based closely on a storytime written by Elizabeth Turner.

 Notes

Monkeys

Anticipated Length: 30 Minutes

Opening:

"**H**ello everyone. My name is Ashley. I am very glad that you came to join me at the library today. I would love lots of participation from both adults and little ones. We are going to begin by singing a great Hello song, so everyone join in and give a great big wave hello to one another."

Opening Song:

Hello Everybody

http://www.peterandellen.com/lyrics/helloeverybody.mp3

(Depending on the size of the group you can then repeat the song substituting each child's name for the word "everybody" in the song.)

Discussion:

Today we will be talking about an animal that swings from the trees and loves to eat bananas (does impression of monkey and makes monkey sounds until kids shout out the correct answer). Yes, a monkey is right. Can we all pretend to be monkeys? Good job, looks like we have some good monkeys in here. We are definitely ready to monkey around!

Book Activity:

Mimi's Book of Counting by Emma Chichester. ISBN#1570915733

Song Activity:

(Have children act out the song's lyrics.)

Teasing Mr. Crocodile

http://www.dltk-teach.com/rhymes/crocodile/words.htm

(This rhyme can be done with puppets. An alligator puppet and five little homemade Popsicle stick monkey puppets work well. Also, you could take an old brown gardening glove, affix Velcro to the fingertips and make monkeys from brown pompoms and googly eyes.)

Activity:

Monkey Puppets

1. Draw or print a monkey on to brown construction paper and cut. http://www.freekidcrafts.com/monkeypuppetc.html
2. Color a monkey and (with help) glue or tape a popsicle stick to the back of it.

Book Activity:
Ten Naughty Little Monkeys by Suzanne Williams. ISBN#9780060599041
Students use their puppets to act as the following book as its read.

Closing Song:
Goodbye Everybody
http://www.peterandellen.com/lyrics/helloeverybody.mp3
(Same tune as Hello Everybody song, but you say, "Goodbye," and "See you soon")

This storytime is based closely on a storytime written by Ashley Sealy.

 Notes

Ocean and Sharing

Anticipated Length: 30 Minutes

Opening:

"Hi Everyone, welcome to today's storytime! Thanks for coming. We are going to be doing a lot of jumping around, so don't stay too glued to your seat! Today we are going to be talking about the ocean and sharing. Let's get started!"

Opening Song:
(Have children act out the song's lyrics.)
Story Hour
http://www.thebestkidsbooksite.com/fingerplays-for-kids.cfm

Book Activity:
In The Ocean (Nature Trails) by A. J. Wood and Maurice Pledger. ISBN# 1571454535

Song Activity:
(Have children act out the song's lyrics.)
Ocean Motion
http://www.thebestkidsbooksite.com/fingerplays-for-kids.cfm

Book Activity:
Sharing a Shell by Julia Donaldson. ISBN#1405020482

Activity:
Sharing the Wealth
Students are given a selection of seashells. They get to pick their favorite to keep and they put this one to the side. Then each of the other children get to pick one from their "leftover" pile. Finally when each child has shared with everyone else, they will each be left with a small pile of seashells they truly like.

Song Activity:
Waves in the Sea
(To the Tune of: "Wheels on the Bus")

> The waves on the sea go up and down, (raise and lower arms)
> Up and down, up and down,
> The waves on the sea go up and down
> All day long

Additional Verses:
The shark in the sea goes snap snap snap . . . (clap your hands)
The fish in the sea go swish swish swish . . . (swish back and forth)
The boats in the sea go toot toot toot . . . (make blowing horn motion)

http://www.thebestkidsbooksite.com/fingerplays-for-kids.cfm
http://kindergarten2.homestead.com/Ocean.html
Continue with additional verses such as . . .

The Sharks in the sea go chomp, chomp, chomp!
The Fishes in the sea go swim, swim, swim!
The Lobsters in the sea go pinch, pinch, pinch!
The Octopus in the sea go wiggle, wiggle, wiggle!
The Seahorse in the sea rock back and forth, back and forth, back and forth!
The Whale in the sea goes squirt, squirt, squirt!
The clam in the sea goes open and shut, open and shut, open and shut!
The crabs in the sea go click, click, click!
The dolphin the sea go jump, jump, jump!

Closing Rhyme:
Storytime's Over
http://www.thebestkidsbooksite.com/fingerplays-for-kids.cfm

Closing to Parents:
All sorts of books on oceans and learning how to share are on the back table if you want more information or items to take home. See you next week!

This storytime was written by Stephanie G. Bauman.

Teddy Bear Picnic

Anticipated Length: 45 Minutes

Opening:

"Good morning boys and girls. I am so glad that you came today. My name is Mrs. Turner. We are going to have lots of fun today, reading together, singing songs, playing games, and doing crafts. Sometimes you will get to play and sometimes you will have to be quiet and listen. When I stand up you can play but when I sit you have to be quiet and listen. Let's practice. (Stand up and tell them to stand up and wiggle. Sit down and have them all sit down. But make it a game. Praise those that catch on.) Parents if at any time your child does not want to participate feel free to take them out and bring them back whenever they are ready. Okay, let's all stand up and sing our first song."

Opening Song:

If You're Happy and You Know It
http://www.kididdles.com/lyrics/i007.html

(My last verse is a quiet last verse.)
If you're happy and you know it, sit like this. (Model the way you want them to sit for the story.)

Discussion:
I see many of you brought your teddy bears to our Teddy Bear Picnic. Now the teddy bears do not know how to act in the library, so it is your job to teach them how to act. I hope you and your teddy bears enjoy our first story today. It is called *Brown Bear, Brown Bear, What Do You See?* Are you ready? Show me my good listeners.

Book Activity:
Brown Bear, Brown Bear, What Do You See? by Bill Martin, Jr., Illus. Eric Carle. ISBN# 0805047905

Song Activity:
(Have children act out the song's lyrics.)
Teddy Bear, Teddy Bear
http://www.songsforteaching.com/nurseryrhymes/teddybearteddybear.htm

Book Activity:
Corduroy by Don Freeman. ISBN# 0590725289

Song Activity:
(Have children act out the song's lyrics.)
Hibernating Bear
http://www.thebestkidsbooksite.com/funfingerplay.cfm?fingerplayid=468
http://www.thebestkidsbooksite.com/fingerplays-for-kids.cfm

Closing Song:
Time to Say Goodbye by Jean Warren
http://www.preschoolexpress.com/music_station03/music_station_may03.shtml
(Tune: "Up on the House Top")

Activity:
Teddy Bear Picnic
(Provide real or fake juice and treats for children and their bears to have a picnic with.)
Make a Corduroy Bear
Have a simple black outline of corduroy bear for the children to color. You will also need crayons, glue, buttons, and corduroy fabric in a variety of colors cut into the shape and size of overalls to fit the bear on the coloring sheet. Children color the bear and then, with help of parents and volunteers, glue the overalls on their color sheet. Once the overalls are on the bear each child will glue on two buttons to finish the project.

This storytime is based closely on a storytime written by Elizabeth Turner.

Transportation

Anticipated Length: 30 Minutes

Opening:
(Blow a train whistle to signal that it's time to start.)

"Hello everybody, my name is Josh. Thanks for coming to storytime. Today we are going to be talking about ways to get from here to there like trains, buses, and trucks. Let's start with a song."

Opening Song:
Hands Go Up and Down (Opening Version) (Sung to: "Twinkle Twinkle Little Star")

> Hands go up and hands go down,
> I can turn around and round.
> I can jump upon two shoes.
> I can listen; so can you.
> I can sit.
> I'll show you how.
> Storytime is starting now.

http://www.carmel.lib.in.us/child/view.cfm?idnum=158
http://ysostorytime.pbworks.com/Storytime-Openings-and-Closings

Book Activity:
Tom's Train by Debbie MacKinnon. ISBN# 0803721056.

Song Activity:
(Have children act out the song's lyrics.)
Down By the Station from the CD *I Love to Sing with Barney*
http://www.tower.com/i-love-sing-barney-cd/wapi/106423313

Book Activity:
Maisy Drives the Bus by Lucy Cousins. ISBN# 0763610836

Song Activity:
(Have children act out the song's lyrics.)
Choo-Choo Train
http://www.thebestkidsbooksite.com/funfingerplay.cfm?fingerplayid=44
http://www.thebestkidsbooksite.com/fingerplays-for-kids.cfm

Book Activity:
My Truck is Stuck by Kevin Lewis. ISBN# 078680534X.

Closing Song:
Hands Go Up and Down (Closing Version)

> Hands go up and hands go down.
> I can turn round and round.
> I can jump upon two shoes.
> I can clap and so can you!
> I can wave,
> I'll show you how.
> Storytime is done for now.

http://ysostorytime.pbworks.com/Storytime-Openings-and-Closings
(Note: See the last song at the bottom of the screen for correct version.)

(Blow the train whistle to signal the end of storytime and the beginning of playtime.)

Closing to Parents:
Thank you all for coming to storytime today. I hope to see you again next week! Parents, I have left books and resources on transportation of all types on the back table.

This storytime is based closely on a storytime written by Joshua Mitchell.

Turtles and Numbers

Anticipated Length: 25 Minutes

Opening:

"Hi everyone, welcome to today's storytime! Thanks for coming. We are going to be doing a lot of jumping around, so don't stay too glued to your seat! Today we are going to be talking about turtles and counting! Let's get started!"

Opening Song:
(Have children act out the song's lyrics.)
Story Hour
http://www.thebestkidsbooksite.com/fingerplays-for-kids.cfm

Song Activity: (Have children act out the song's lyrics.)
Turtle Teapot
(To the Tune of: "I'm a Little Teapot")
http://www.thebestkidsbooksite.com/fingerplays-for-kids.cfm

Book Activity:
Turtle Splash! Countdown at the Pond by Cathryn Falwell. ISBN# 0060294620

Song Activity: (Have children act out the song's lyrics.)
Turtles

> One baby turtle alone and new.
> Finds a friend, and then there are two.
> Two baby turtles crawl down to the sea.
> They find another, and then there are three.
> Three baby turtles crawl along the shore.
> They find another, and then there are four.
> Four baby turtles go for a dive.
> Up swims another, and then there are five.

http://www.preschoolrainbow.org/preschool-rhymes.htm

Book Activity:
Ten Tiny Turtles: A Crazy Counting Book by Paul Cherrill. ISBN# 0395712505

Closing Song:
Storytime's Over
http://www.thebestkidsbooksite.com/fingerplays-for-kids.cfm

Closing to Parents:

This is an ideal time to start learning simple numbers and counting. Give your children a reason to learn to count, make it something relevant and worthwhile to them, like letting them count out yummy berries to put in their cereal.If you want more information about helping your children learn simple numbers or all about turtles, additional materials are on the back table. See you next week!

This storytime was written by Stephanie G. Bauman.

 Notes

3

Tykes (5–6 Year Olds)

These Tykes are children of the entertainment age, so it is essential to be ready with a great storytime that includes engaging activities. Action verses are recommended to help divert some of that high energy level. This age group is ready for verses that challenge with motion, such as fast directions like left, right, up, and down, as well as more complicated songs that can be acted out, such as hiding and yawning.

Just starting their formal education, this naturally inquisitive group will like storytimes that are a bit more challenging, with time for all their many questions! They want to know about the things *they like*: dinosaurs, imaginary creatures, pirates, and adventures. They also want to be a central part of the story, so make sure the characters are those that the Tykes can identify with. Activities where they can take something home like a pet rock or a paper kite will have them anticipating future storytimes. These items will also help them with retention of the lessons from that day. Just make sure that these activities do not include food unless you have parent permission. This is a great age for storytimes because the children are still young enough to think it's great when you are silly and the story plots and themes are more interesting and engaging for you as well.

Astronauts and Career Exploration

Anticipated Length: 45 Minutes

Opening:

"Hi everyone, welcome to today's storytime! Thanks for coming. We are going to be doing a lot of jumping around, so don't stay too glued to your seat! Today we are going to be talking about everyone's favorite: outer space! Let's get started!"

Opening Song:
(Have children act out the song's lyrics.)
Story Hour
http://www.thebestkidsbooksite.com/fingerplays-for-kids.cfm

Discussion:
Outer space is such a neat place. Can you imagine worlds full of people like us or not like us living their lives and playing in their distant worlds? Maybe someday soon we can travel there! Or maybe someday they will come see us! If you could get in a spaceship and live on another planet would you?

Book Activity:
Here In Space by David Milgrim. ISBN# 0816744629

Song Activity:
(Have children act out the song's lyrics.)
The Hokey Space Pokey version by Stephanie G. Bauman

> I bring the astronaut in, I send the astronaut out
> I bring the astronaut in and I fly him/her all about
> I do the funky moonwalk and turn myself around,
> That's what space is all about!
> I spy a milky way here, I spy a milky way there (pointing)
> I fly to the milky way and sprinkle chocolate all about (flying and sprinkling)
> I shake up the milky way and turn myself around,
> That what chocolate milks all about!
> I saw an alien here, I saw an alien there!
> I saw an alien here so I got my laser pointer out.
> I chased him all across the galaxy then turned myself around.
> That's what alien chases are all about!
> I send out a shooting star here, I send out a shooting star there!
> I send out shooting stars flying everywhere!

I send out shooting starts until my cannon's all out!
That's what creating galaxies is all about!

Book Activity:
Me and My Place in Space by Joan Sweeney. ISBN# 0517885905

Closing Song:
Storytime's Over
http://www.thebestkidsbooksite.com/fingerplays-for-kids.cfm

Closing to Parents:
If you or your children want more information or items to take home, there are books on astronauts, space exploration, and stars are on the back table.

This storytime was written by Stephanie G. Bauman.

 Notes

Our Bodies

Anticipated Length: 45 Minutes

Opening:

"Hi everyone, welcome to today's storytime! Thanks for coming. We are going to be doing a lot of jumping around, so don't stay too glued to your seat! Today we are going to be talking about the body! Let's get started!"

Opening Song:
(Have children act out the song's lyrics.)
Story Hour
http://www.thebestkidsbooksite.com/fingerplays-for-kids.cfm

Book Activity:
Me and My Body by Joan Sweeney. ISBN# 0375806237

Song Activity:
(Have children act out the song's lyrics.)
Head, Shoulders, Knees, and Toes
http://www.songsforteaching.com/learningstation/headshoulders.htm

Book Activity:
I Want to Be Somebody New! by Robert Lopshire. ISBN#0394876164

Book Activity:
The Skin You Live In by Michael Tyler. ISBN# 0975958003

Discussion:
Our bodies are really interesting and lots of fun to move when we dance! Everyone has a different body? Wouldn't the world be a boring place if everyone looked the same? (Use the remaining questions until interest in the discussion stops.)
Let's think about the way we use the parts of our bodies.

Why do we need eyes?

Why do we need ears?

Why do we have a nose?

What happens to your nose when you have a cold or an allergy to something?

Which is the hand you use to hold a crayon to color?

Where do you usually need to put a Band-Aid?

Why do you need feet?

Why do we cover our feet?

Closing Song:

Storytime's Over

http://www.thebestkidsbooksite.com/fingerplays-for-kids.cfm

Closing to Parents:

More books on the human body and accepting differences in self and others are on the back table for you and your children to look at or check out to take home.

Additional Activity Ideas:

Talk about ways to make everyone feel included and accepted.

Talk about similarities. How are the children the same?

This storytime was written by Stephanie G. Bauman.

 Notes

Creepy Crawlies

Anticipated Length: 45 Minutes

Opening:

"Hello everyone. My name is Ashley. I am very glad that you came to join me at the library today. I would love lots of participation from both adults and little ones. We are going to begin by singing a great Hello song, so everyone join in and give a great big wave hello to one another."

Opening Song:

Hello Everybody
http://www.peterandellen.com/lyrics/helloeverybody.mp3
(Depending on the size of the group you can then repeat the song substituting each child's name for the word "everybody" in the song.)

Discussion:
Today we will be talking all about bugs. Can you think of some different kinds of bugs you have seen? What about a caterpillar? Caterpillars look a little like worms, but then what do they turn into? That's right, beautiful butterflies! How many of you would like to eat bugs? No way . . . me neither. But, the first book we are going to read is all about someone who is very greedy and loves to eat bugs.

Book Activity:
The Roly Poly Spider by Jill Sardegna. ISBN# 0590471198

Song Activity:
(Have children act out the song's lyrics.)
The Eensy Weensy Spider
http://www.kididdles.com/lyrics/e001.html
(Repeat song with teeny tiny spider [using high-pitched, tiny voice] and big fat spider [using deep, booming voice]).

Song Activity:
(Have children act out the song's lyrics.)
The Ants Go Marching
http://www.kididdles.com/lyrics/a009.html

Activity:
Butterfly Masks

Cut out a half-face, masquerade-style mask shape from construction paper in a wide variety of colors. Have the children color them like beautiful butterflies. Glue or tape a popsicle stick or chopstick to the side so that they can hold the mask to their face.

Closing to Parents:
I hope you enjoyed storytime today. There are lots of books about different kinds of creepy crawlies if you would like to take one home with you today. I love all of the colorful butterfly masks that I see. With your new masks you can pretend to be a caterpillar on the floor and then change into a beautiful butterfly to fly away home. If you have any questions or would like some help finding some materials to take home, please let me know.

Closing Song:
Goodbye Everybody
http://www.peterandellen.com/lyrics/helloeverybody.mp3
(Same tune as Hello Everybody song, but you say Goodbye and See you Soon).

This storytime is based closely on a storytime written by Ashley Sealy.

 Notes

Dr. Seuss

Anticipated Length: 45 Minutes

Opening:

"**G**ood afternoon everyone. I am so glad you all came. My name is Mrs. Turner. Are you ready to read some stories and have some fun? Okay. Show me my good listeners. Good listeners are sitting criss-cross applesauce, hands in your lap. (Demonstrate how you expect them to sit.)"

Opening Song:

Open, Shut Them
http://www.kididdles.com/lyrics/o027.html

Discussion:
Boys and girls, the stories that I am going to share with you today are all by the same author and illustrator. The author is Dr. Seuss. He is very famous and he wrote a lot of books. The illustrator is Dr. Seuss, too. Remember the author is the person that writes the words and the illustrator is the person that draws the pictures. One thing that is fun about Dr. Seuss books is the rhyming words. It is very hard for me to read Dr. Seuss books out loud because I get so tongue tied. I think you should ask your parents to read you some Dr. Seuss books and see if they get tongue tied too.

Book Activity:
Horton Hears A Who by Dr. Seuss. ISBN# 9780394800783

Song Activity:
(Have children act out the song's lyrics.)
Green Eggs and Ham Song
http://www.songsforteaching.com/classicalchildrensliterature/greeneggsandham.htm

Activity:
Attention Focus
If you can hear me, touch your _____.

Book Activity:
The Lorax by Dr. Seuss. ISBN #978039423379

Song Activity:
(Have children act out the song's lyrics.)
I've Got a Wiggle
http://www.songsforteaching.com/cathybollinger/s/wiggle.mp3

Activity:
Green Eggs and Ham Tic Tac Toe
Children can make their own, or you can provide laminated tic tac toe boards for re-use.

Closing Song:
Heigh Ho from the Snow White Soundtrack.
http://www.stlyrics.com/songs/s/snowwhiteandthesevendwarfs21817/heighho564894.html

Closing to Parents:
Dr. Seuss's birthday is March 2 and librarians across the United States celebrate his birthday with a program: Read Across America. You may have older brothers and sisters who are helping celebrate this birthday at their schools as they Read Across America. We have many Dr. Seuss books and some that are very similar if you love tongue-twisting rhymes. They are at the table in the back for you to choose one to take home with you today.

This storytime is based closely on a storytime written by Elizabeth Turner

Earth Day

Anticipated Length: 45 Minutes

Opening:

"Welcome to storytime! My name is Julie and I want to welcome you all to the library today. This week, we are thinking about Earth Day. It takes place every year on April 22. The Earth is the name of our planet and Earth Day is a day when we celebrate and think about ways to keep it beautiful. Let's get started!"

Opening Song:

The More We Get Together
http://www.songsforteaching.com/jimrule/themorewegettogether.htm

Book Activity:
The Water Hole by Graeme Base. ISBN# 0810945681

Discussion:
The Earth has only so much water to share with all the people and animals. We should be careful not to waste water. What are some ways that we can be careful with water? Here's a rhyme about a critter that likes to live in the water.

Song Activity:
(Have children act out the song's lyrics.)
I Had a Little Turtle
http://bussongs.com/songs/i_had_a_little_turtle.php

Song Activity:
(Have children act out the song's lyrics.)
Recycling Song
http://www.songsforteaching.com/geofjohnson/recycle.htm

Book Activity:
The Rose In My Garden by Arnold Lobel. ISBN# 0688122655

Song Activity:
(Have children act out the song's lyrics.)
Everyday an Earth Day by Ron Brown
http://www.songsforteaching.com/intellitunes/earthdaysong.htm

Activity:
Planting Tree Seeds
Supplies: Recycled food containers, potting soil, seeds, markers to decorate containers
Every tree helps clean the air we breathe. So today, we are planting trees in some recycled containers. You can take them home and watch your little trees grow. When they are bigger, you can plant them outside. Caregivers, please help your children with the planting of the seeds. Please pick up a story list and take the time to browse around before you leave. The library has all kinds of great books about taking care of our earth both for kids and grownups!

Closing Song:
I'm so glad we had this time together
http://cantgitsngoutmyhead.spaces.live.com/Blog/cns!DF71074B7E1EFE00!533.entry

This storytime is based closely on a storytime written by Julie Andrews-Jotham.

 Notes

Farm and Food

Anticipated Length: 45 Minutes

Opening:

"Hi everyone, welcome to today's storytime! Thanks for coming. We are going to be doing a lot of jumping around, so don't stay too glued to your seat! Today we are going to be talking about food and some ideas about where it comes from. Let's get started!"

Opening Song:
(Have children act out the song's lyrics.)
Story Hour
http://www.thebestkidsbooksite.com/fingerplays-for-kids.cfm

Book Activity:
Life on a Crop Farm by Judy Wolfman. ISBN# 157505518X

Discussion:
We aren't the only thing that likes to eat up all this good food, so do all the animals that live near the farm. Farmers often make a thing called a scarecrow to keep birds from eating all the food, especially the corn. A scarecrow looks like a man who has been made out of straw and dressed in old farm clothes. Today we are going to sing about a scarecrow, so everybody stand up. Try to sing and copy what I do.

Song Activity:
(Have children act out the song's lyrics.)
Scarecrow
(One child is the scarecrow in the middle of the circle. The other children stand.)
From: *Move over Mother Goose* by Ruth McDowell. ISBN# 9780876591130

Book Activity:
Cloudy with a Chance of Meatballs by Judi Barrett. ISBN# 0689707495

Discussion:
Where did the food you have at home come from? What you would do if food was falling instead of rain or snow? What would you grow if you had a farm? You can be a farmer right now. Ask your parents about growing plants in your yard, or in pots in the windowsill.

Activity:
Plant a Bean
Children get to plant a bean in something such as a small pot, a can, or egg carton bits.

Closing Song:
Storytime's Over
http://www.thebestkidsbooksite.com/fingerplays-for-kids.cfm

Closing to Parents:
Books on farms, food, and gardening are on the back table if you want more information or items to take home. Thanks for coming today, see you next week!

Additional Activity Ideas:

> A guest speaker from a community garden could be invited. Parents may want to get involved with their kids! Start a small garden on the library grounds or in a large window in the children's section.

This storytime was written by Stephanie G. Bauman.

Fire Safety and Awareness

Anticipated Length: 45 Minutes

Opening:

"**H**ello everyone! My name is Josh. Thanks for coming to storytime today. Today we are going to learn more about safety. Let's get started by singing our welcome song."

Opening Song:

Welcome, Welcome
http://wiki.kcls.org/tellmeastory/index.php/Welcome_Welcome_Everyone
http://librarydiaries.blogspot.com/2006/06/pre-school-story-time.html
(Tune of Twinkle Twinkle Little Star)

Book Activity:
No Dragons for Tea: Fire Safety for Kids (and Dragons) by Jean Pendziwol. ISBN# 1550745697

Book Activity:
A Day in the Life of a Firefighter by Heather Adamson. ISBN# 0736822844

Song Activity:
(Have children act out the song's lyrics.)
Down at the Firehouse (Tune of "Down by the Station")

> Down at the firehouse
> Early in the morning,
> You can see our clothes
> Hanging in a row.
> When there is a fire,
> We can dress real fast.
> Boots, jackets, hats, gloves,
> Off we go!

http://www.preschoolsings.citymax.com/communitysongs.html

Book Activity:
Do You Smell Smoke? A Story about Safety with Fire by Cindy Leaney. ISBN# 1589527410

Song Activity:
(Have children act out the song's lyrics.)
Fire Safety by Leora Grecian from *The Piggyback Songbook* (Tune of "Frère Jacques")
http://www.hummingbirded.com/fire.html

Activity:
Fire Engine Art Project
Precut circle and rectangle shapes out of construction paper. Have children use glue to create fire engines. Yarn can be used for the fire hose and straws for the ladder. Color and decorate.
http://www.hummingbirded.com/fire.html

Closing to Parents:
There is no better time for your children to learn about emergency safety, fire included. Having knowledge like this can help a child throughout their entire life, and give them a feeling of pride to know that they are prepared. I have placed books on fire, emergency safety, and some Smokey the Bear bookmarks on the back table.

Additional Activity Ideas:

Invite a guest speaker from a local fire department.

This storytime is based closely on a storytime written by Joshua Mitchell.

Friendship

Anticipated Length: 45 Minutes

Opening:

"**G**ood afternoon everyone. I am so glad you all came. My name is Mrs. Turner. Are you ready to read some stories and have some fun? Okay. Show me my good listeners. Good listeners are sitting criss-cross applesauce, hands in your lap. (Demonstrate how you expect them to sit.)"

Opening Song:

Open, Shut Them
http://www.kididdles.com/lyrics/o027.html

Book Activity:

The Remarkable Friendship of Mr. Cat and Mr. Rat by Rick Walton and Lisa McCue. ISBN# 0399238999
(I use an Elmo connected to a computer, an LCD projector and screen. The book goes under the Elmo and it projects the page onto the screen.)

Song Activity:

You've Got a Friend in Me by Randy Newman
http://www.youtube.com/watch?v=LXARdPb4YBs

Book Activity:

How to Be a Friend: A Guide to Making Friends and Keeping Them by Laurie K Brown. ISBN# 0316111538

Closing Song:

Heigh Ho from the Snow White Sound Track.
http://www.stlyrics.com/songs/s/snowwhiteandthesevendwarfs21817/heighho564894.html

Closing to Parents:

On the back table I have set out a selection of books about friendship. Please feel free to check out as many as you'd like.

Additional Activity Ideas:

Practice making new friends. The children pretend they are strangers and meet each other. Or two classes from the same grade could meet. In a public library the children could introduce themselves to all the librarians at the reference desks.

This storytime is based closely on a storytime written by Elizabeth Turner.

Grandparents

Anticipated Length: 30 Minutes

Opening:

"Hello, my name is Jake. I'm glad you all could join us here today. Today we're going to talk about grandparents. Your grandparents are the mommy and daddy . . . of your mommy and daddy! Do we have any grandmas and grandpas here with us today? I hope so. Today we're going to read some stories and sing some songs about grandmas and grandpas. Let's get started with our hello song!"

Opening Song:
Good Morning by Greg and Steve (We All Live Together Vol. 2 CD)

Book Activity:
The Hello, Goodbye Window by Norman Juster and Chris Raschka. ISBN# 0786809140

Song Activity:
(Have children act out the song's lyrics.)
Grandma's Glasses/Grandpa's Glasses

> These are grandma's glasses. (Make circles around eyes.)
> This is grandma's hat. (Cup hands and place on head.)
> And this is the way
> She folds her hands (Fold hands)
> And puts them in her lap. (Put hands in your lap.)
> These are grandpa's glasses. (Make circles around eyes.)
> This is grandpa's hat. (Pretend to put on a hat.)
> And this is the way
> He folds his arms (Cross arms and fold.)
> Just like that!

http://www.drjean.org/html/monthly_act/act_2008/01_Jan/pg01.html
http://www.songsforteaching.com/fingerplays/grandmasglasses.htm

Book Activity:
Lunchtime for a Purple Snake by Harriet Ziefert and Todd McKie. ISBN:# 0618311335

Song Activity:
(Have children act out the song's lyrics.)
Shake My Sillies Out by Raffi (More Singable Songs CD)
http://www.metrolyrics.com/shake-my-sillies-out-lyrics-raffi.html

Song Activity:
(Have children act out the song's lyrics.)
Shout and Whisper
http://www.babysongs.com/pages.cfm?ID=19

Book Activity
What Grandmas Do Best/What Grandpas Do Best by Laura Numeroff and Lynn Munsinger. ISBN# 0689805527

Closing Song:
Goodbye by Francine Wheeler (Come Sit Beside Me CD)

Closing to Parents:
I have some books about grandparents on the table in the back of the room. Feel free to take them home with you today. Or if you need help finding some other books that you think you'll enjoy, please come talk to me. I hope you've had a good time, and that you'll come see us again next week.

This storytime is based closely on a storytime written by Jake Sexton.

Halloween

Anticipated Length: 45 Minutes

Opening:

"Hello everyone. My name is Ashley. I am very glad that you came to join me at the library today. We are going to begin by singing a great Hello song, so everyone join in and give a great big wave hello to one another."

Opening Song:

Welcome, Welcome
http://wiki.kcls.org/tellmeastory/index.php/Welcome_Welcome_Everyone
(Tune of Twinkle Twinkle Little Star)

Discussion:
A very exciting holiday is coming up. It is a day where you can dress up in a costume and you get candy. What day am I talking about? Today we will be talking about Halloween!

Song Activity:
(Have children act out the song's lyrics.)
Three Little Witches
http://www.kididdles.com/lyrics/t064.html

Book Activity:
Miss Smith and the Haunted Library by Michael Garland. ISBN# 0525421394

Song Activity:
(Have children act out the song's lyrics.)
Pumpkin on the Ground

Pumpkin, pumpkin on the ground (crouch down)
How'd you get so big and round? (stretch arms out wide to sides and then make a circle)
Once you were a seed so small, (pretend to hold a seed)
Now you are a great big ball! (make huge circle with hands)
Pumpkin, pumpkin on the ground (crouch down)
How'd you get so big and round? (stretch arms out wide to sides and then make a circle)

http://www.thebestkidsbooksite.com/fingerplays-for-kids.cfm

Book Activity:
In a Dark Dark House by Neil Labute. ISBN# 9780865479562

Activity:
Poor Joe Interactive Storytelling
http://www.angelfire.com/ca4/SnugglyBug/campfirestories/poorjoe.html

Closing Song:
The End from Early literacy storytimes @ your library: partnering with caregivers for success by Saroj Nadkarni Ghoting and Pamela Martin-Díaz
(Tune of Twinkle Twinkle Little Star)
http://is.gd/5hf7M

Closing to Parents:
Thanks for coming in today! We have lots of spooky books in this library! If you like ghosts, goblins, or even witches come and check out some great reads!

Additional Activity Ideas:

Pumpkin painting, on tiny pumpkins for each child.
Face painting, in Halloween creations.
How Halloween is celebrated in other countries.

This storytime based closely on a storytime written by Ashley Sealy.

Hibernation/Migration

Anticipated Length: 45 Minutes

Opening:

"**H**ello everyone. My name is Ashley. I am very glad that you came to join me at the library today. We are going to begin by singing a great Hello song, so everyone join in and give a great big wave hello to one another."

Opening Song:

Welcome, Welcome
http://wiki.kcls.org/tellmeastory/index.php/Welcome_Welcome_Everyone
(Tune of Twinkle Twinkle Little Star)

Discussion:

When it's cold outside we all snuggle up together in our warm house in front of the fireplaces (if you have a fireplace) and blankets. But what do animals do when its winter? Do you know what hibernation is? It is when some animals, like bears go into a deep sleep all winter. Would you like to sleep all winter? Other animals hibernate too, like skunks. Some kinds of bird fly to warmer places, wouldn't that be nice? It's called migration.

Book Activity:

Bear Snores On by Karma Wilson. ISBN# 0689831870.

Song Activity:

(Have children act out the song's lyrics.)
Hibernating Bear

> Here is a cave. (bend fingers to form cave)
> Inside is a bear. (put thumb inside fingers)
> Now he comes out. (thumb out)
> To get some fresh air.
> He stays out all summer
> In sunshine and heat.
> He hunts in the forest
> For berries to eat. (Move thumb in circle.)
> When snow starts to fall
> He hurries inside.
> His warm little cave (thumb in)
> And there he will hide.
> Snow covers the cave

From *Storytimes for Children* by Stephanie G. Bauman. Santa Barbara, CA: Libraries Unlimited. Copyright © 2011.

Like a fluffy white rug. (Cover with other hand.)
Inside the bear sleeps
All cozy and snug.

http://www.thebestkidsbooksite.com/funfingerplay.cfm?fingerplayid=468
http://www.thebestkidsbooksite.com/fingerplays-for-kids.cfm

Book Activity:
Duck at the Door by Jackie Urbanovic. ISBN# 9870061214387

Song Activity:
(Have children act out the song's lyrics.)
Bird Migration by David Burba
http://www.songsforteaching.com/animalsongs/birdmigration.htm

Closing Song:
The End from Early literacy storytimes @ your library: partnering with caregivers for success by Saroj Nadkarni Ghoting and Pamela Martin-Díaz
(Tune of Twinkle Twinkle Little Star)
http://is.gd/5hf7M

Closing to Parents:
I am so glad you came to storytime today! We had a lot of fun talking about hibernation today! I wish I could fly south for the winter like a bird. We have lots of fun books at the library about other migrating creatures like butterflies and whales, so check them out!

This storytime based closely on a storytime written by Ashley Sealy.

Music

Anticipated Length: 30 Minutes

Opening:

"Hello everyone! My name is Josh. Thanks for coming to storytime today. Today's theme is music. Let's get started by singing our welcome song."

Opening Song:

Welcome, Welcome
http://wiki.kcls.org/tellmeastory/index.php/Welcome_Welcome_Everyone
http://librarydiaries.blogspot.com/2006/06/pre-school-story-time.html
(Tune of Twinkle Twinkle Little Star)

Book Activity:
Our Marching Band by Lloyd Moss. ISBN# 0399233350

Book Activity:
Sound and Music by David Evans and Claudette Williams. ISBN# 156458206X

Song Activity:
(Have children act out the song's lyrics.)
When the Band Begins to Play
http://www.kididdles.com/lyrics/w040.html
(Children can march along in time to the music pretending to play their "instruments" as they go.)

Book Activity:
What Instrument Is This? by Rosmarie Hausherr. ISBN# 0590446444

Book Activity:
The Best Mariachi in the World by J.D. Smith. ISBN# 0977090617

Activity:
Make a Kazoo
http://www.thebestkidsbooksite.com/printcraft.cfm?CraftID=1143
Materials needed: paper towel roll or toilet paper roll, a hole puncher, wax paper, scissors, markers, and a rubber band.

Create by punching a hole near one end of your tube. Then cut a medium-sized square of wax paper and bunch it up over the middle of one end, securing with a rubber band. Then the kazoos can be decorated.

Song Activity:
(Have children act out the song's lyrics.)
Good-Bye Song
http://www.songsforteaching.com/happalmer/goodbye.htm
(Pantomime playing each instrument as it is named in the song.)

Closing to Parents:
This is a great time for your children to begin to learn about music. They have a great ear for rhythm, are extra creative, enthusiastic, and are at a learning level where they can learn new instruments more readily. Books on instruments, including a few on creating your own as well as some literature about music lessons offered at the local community center are on the table in the back of the room.

This storytime is based closely on a storytime written by Joshua Mitchell.

 Notes

Pirates

Anticipated Length: 45 Minutes

Opening:

"Hi everyone, welcome to today's storytime! Thanks for coming. We are going to be doing a lot of jumping around, so don't stay too glued to your seat! Today we are going to be talking about PIRATES! Let's get started!"

Opening Song:
(Have children act out the song's lyrics.)
Story Hour
http://www.thebestkidsbooksite.com/fingerplays-for-kids.cfm

Discussion:
Did you know there are still real pirates on the sea! Off the coast of a country called Somalia, many ships have been taken by sea pirates. Read parts of articles such as:
http://www.cbsnews.com/stories/2008/11/21/world/main4624453.shtml

Book Activity:
How I Became a Pirate by Melinda Long. ISBN# 0152018484

Song Activity:
(Have children act out the song's lyrics.)
Fierce Pirate

I'm a fierce pirate, (Brandish sword or dagger)
Captain of my ship. (Stand at attention)
I stride the deck (Walk in place)
With hand on hip. (Put hands on hips)
Our big black flag shows a skull and cross bones. (Hands over eyes, or look through telescope)
Everybody moans. (Throw up hands and moan)
Out of the hold dark and dank, (Climb ladder with hands)
We bring the captive (Hands together behind back)
Who walks the plank. (Walk fingers of one hand off index finger of the other hand)
Without our gold and silver,
Away we go with many a SHOUT (Cup hands around mouth)
And a YO-HO-HO! (Say loudly)

http://www.thebestkidsbooksite.com/fingerplays-for-kids.cfm

Book Activity:
Pirate Pete's Talk like a Pirate by Kim Kennedy. ISBN# 0810993481

Activity:
Talk Like a Pirate
Create a handout of pirate words from the following Web site and practice saying them. Hand out prizes for best pirate speech. (Give everyone a bookmark.)
http://www.thepiratesrealm.com/pirate%20talk.html

Closing Song:
Storytime's Over
http://www.thebestkidsbooksite.com/fingerplays-for-kids.cfm

Closing to Parents:
Books on pirates, the navy, the ocean, and ships are on the back table if you want more information or items to check out and take home.

Additional Activity Ideas:

Movie: Scooby-Doo in *Pirates Ahoy!* 2006
Movie: *Muppet Treasure Island*—Kermit's 50th Anniversary Edition 2005
Create eye patches.
Have a guest speaker come with a parrot.

This storytime was written by Stephanie G. Bauman.

Seasons

Anticipated Length: 45 Minutes

Opening:

"Hello everyone! My name is Josh. Thanks for coming to storytime today. Today we are going to learn more about the seasons. Let's get started by singing our welcome song."

Opening Song:

Welcome, Welcome
http://wiki.kcls.org/tellmeastory/index.php/Welcome_Welcome_Everyone
http://librarydiaries.blogspot.com/2006/06/pre-school-story-time.html
(Tune of "Twinkle Twinkle Little Star")

Book Activity:
All Year Long by Kathleen Deady. ISBN# 1575055376

Song Activity:
(Have children act out the song's lyrics.)
Spring is Showery

Spring is showery, flowery, bowery,
Summer is hoppy, croppy, poppy.
Autumn is slippy, drippy, nippy,
Winter is breezy, sneezy, freezy.

http://www.thebestkidsbooksite.com/supersongs.cfm?songsid=296
http://www.thebestkidsbooksite.com/fingerplays-for-kids.cfm

Book Activity:
Riddles about the Seasons by Jacqueline Ball. ISBN# 0671685821
(Read excerpts).

Song Activity:
(Have children act out the song's lyrics.)
Four Seasons by Jeff Schroeder
http://www.songsforteaching.com/jeffschroeder/4seasons.htm

Book Activity:
A Bear for All Seasons by Diane Marcial Fuchs. ISBN# 0805021396

Activity:
Summer Lily
http://www.thebestkidsbooksite.com/printcraft.cfm?CraftID=563
The child's handprint is cut out of colored paper. Fold the thumb and pinky together to form a cone shape. For a stem, insert a green piece of pipe cleaner into the base on the flower. For leaves create green paper leaves to wrap and glue in place.

Closing to Parents:
Learning about the seasons can be fun and interesting. If your child is interested in learning more, I have put some books on the back table about the four seasons, including a few on legends and the origins of seasonal holidays.

Additional Activity Ideas:

> Make snowflakes by folding up white paper and making random scissor cuts.
> Make cutouts of autumn leaves, or pressed leaves.
> Talk more about the animals of the four seasons.
> Learn about hibernation. (See suggested storytime earlier in this section.)
> Learn more about the sports of the four seasons.

This storytime is based closely on a storytime written by Joshua Mitchell.

Shapes

Anticipated Length: 45 Minutes

Opening:

"Hello everyone. My name is Ashley. I am very glad that you came to join me at the library today. I would love lots of participation from both adults and tykes. We are going to begin by singing a great Hello song, so everyone join in and give a great big wave hello to one another."

Opening Song:

Hello Everybody
http://www.peterandellen.com/lyrics/helloeverybody.mp3
(Depending on the size of the group you can then repeat the song substituting each child's name for the word "everybody" in the song.)

Discussion:
We are going to be looking at all sorts of different shapes today. What are some of the shapes that you can think of? Can you see any of them right here in this room?

Activity:
Name That Shape
Have felt board and felt shapes. Before each shape, sing the song and have children successfully guess the name of the shape before placing it on the board. (Sing to **What Shape Is This?**) http://www.uen.org/lessonplan/upload/10715-2-14434-shape_poem _songs.pdf
(Sung to "Do You Know The Muffin Man? ")

Book Activity:
Wings of a Flea: A Book about Shapes by Ed Emberley. ISBN# 0316234877

Song Activity:
(Have children act out the song's lyrics.)
The Shape Hokey Pokey by Debbie Haren
http://www.lessonplanspage.com/MathMusicHokeyPokeyShapesIdeaPK.htm
Give each child five large construction paper shapes in bright colors. Have them select the correct shape as you sing the song together. Repeat with other four shapes, such as green triangle, purple star, and yellow heart.

Book Activity:
Mouse Shapes by Ellen Stoll Walsh. ISBN# 9780152060916

Activity:
Get Creative with Shapes
Give each child a plain piece of paper and a glue stick. Have them choose from a bowl of shape cut-outs and glue them to their paper to make pictures, like the mice did in the book.

Closing Song:
Goodbye Everybody
http://www.peterandellen.com/lyrics/helloeverybody.mp3
(Same tune as Hello Everybody song, but you say Goodbye and See you soon).

Closing to Parents:
Please help your child to pick out the shapes and colors that they see every day. If you have any questions or would like some help finding some materials to take home, please let me know.

This storytime is based closely on a storytime written by Ashley Sealy.

Sharing

Anticipated Length: 45 Minutes

Opening:

"Hi everyone, welcome to today's storytime! Thanks for coming! Today is such a nice day. Let's have some fun stories before you go back out to play! Today we are going to be talking about sharing and working together! Let's get started!"

Opening Song:
(Have children act out the song's lyrics.)
Story Hour
http://www.thebestkidsbooksite.com/fingerplays-for-kids.cfm

Discussion:
Sharing is letting someone else enjoy or use what is yours. It is important to share as much as you can. Imagine if cars didn't share the road with each other, there would be no place to drive. Or if the birds didn't share the sky with each other, all the birds would have to walk but one. Working and sharing together is a fun and important way to make friends. Imagine a big buffet where each person brings their favorite food. Now instead of just one plate of the same food, you can have a bit of everyone's best food.

Book Activity:
Mumkin by Stephen Cosgrove. ISBN# 0843114312

Activity:
Chain Story
We are going to make a story together! Each of us is going to say a few sentences to add to a story that I am going to start. That way each of us can build on a story together and share it. I will write it down and give it to each of you at the end of storytime.

"Once upon a time there was a little bear that wanted to share all he had. He gave a sticky pawful of honey to. . . ."

Discussion:
Not everything should be or can be shared. For instance if you shared all your clothes, you would be super cold!! When is a time it's ok not to share? Let's talk about germs!

Book Activity:
Germs Are Not for Sharing by Elizabeth Verdick. ISBN# 1575421976

From *Storytimes for Children* by Stephanie G. Bauman. Santa Barbara, CA: Libraries Unlimited. Copyright © 2011.

Closing Song:
Storytime's Over
http://www.thebestkidsbooksite.com/fingerplays-for-kids.cfm

Closing to Parents:
Books on sharing and book on germs are on the back table if you want more information or items to take home. See you next week!

This storytime was written by Stephanie G. Bauman.

 Notes

Silly Storytime

Anticipated Length: 45 Minutes

Opening:

“Hello and welcome to our silly storytime! There are sheets here with the words to the songs and a list of silly book suggestions for you to take home. Caregivers, please help the children follow along with the songs and poems. So, let's get started!”

Song Activity:
(Have children act out the song's lyrics.)
Shake My Sillies Out by Raffi [More Singable Songs CD]
http://www.metrolyrics.com/shake-my-sillies-out-lyrics-raffi.html

Book Activity:
A Silly Story by Mercer Mayer. ISBN# 1577683382

Activity:
Tongue Twisters
Here are some silly poems called tongue twisters. They are easy if you say them slowly, but see what happens when you repeat them faster and faster.
http://www.barkingspiderspoetry.com/tonguetwisters.html

Song Activity:
(Have children act out the song's lyrics.)
Head and Shoulders
http://www.kididdles.com/lyrics/h002.html

Book Activity:
Mr. Reeze's Sneezes by Curtis Parkinson. ISBN# 1550375563

Activity:
Clown Puppets

    Each child is invited to color a prepared clown face.

    Cut out the clown faces.

    Glue the faces to the bottom flap of a brown paper bag.

    Glue on pom-pom for clown's nose and other decorations.

    Show and tell with puppets.

    Invite children to give their puppet a name.

Closing to Parents:
Thanks for coming to our silly storytime today! Check out some of our silly books in the children's room, and have your puppet read your parent a story! We'll see you next time!

Closing Song:
The More We Get Together
http://www.songsforteaching.com/jimrule/themorewegettogether.htm

This storytime is based closely on a storytime written by Julie Andrews-Jotham.

 Notes

Snow

Anticipated Length: 45 Minutes

Opening:

"ello everyone. My name is Ashley. I am very glad that you came to join me at the library today. We are going to begin by singing a great Hello song, so everyone join in and give a great big wave hello to one another."

Opening Song:

Hello Everybody
http://www.peterandellen.com/lyrics/helloeverybody.mp3
(Depending on the size of the group you can then repeat the song substituting each child's name for the word "everybody" in the song.)

Discussion:
Did you see the snow on the ground outside today? I think snow is really fun. You can do all sorts of things with it like building a snowman, having a snowball fight, building an igloo, or going sledding.

Book Activity:
The Ice Bear's Cave by Mark Haddon. ISBN# 01405012827

Song Activity:
(Have children act out the song's lyrics.)
Assorted Winter Themed Songs
http://www.canteach.ca/elementary/songspoems7.html
http://is.gd/5iAEn

Discussion:
What do you like to do in the snow? The first book that we are going to read together is about a little boy like you who had a lot of fun in the snow.

Book Activity:
The Snowy Day by Ezra Jack Keats. ISBN# 01405012827

Activity:
Snowman
Create a basic snowman picture on white paper, and then have the children add hat, scarf or anything they would like to the snowman. Finally cover with glue and have the children paste cotton balls all over the snowman's body.

Closing Song:
Goodbye Everybody
http://www.peterandellen.com/lyrics/helloeverybody.mp3
(Same tune as Hello Everybody song, but you say Goodbye and See you Soon).

Closing to Parents:
I am so happy you could make it here today! Snow can be really fun but also really cold, so bundle up if you are going out in it!

Additional Activity Ideas:

Have a fake snowball fight, with Styrofoam balls.

This storytime is based closely on a storytime written by Ashley Sealy.

 Notes

Sports

Anticipated Length: 30 Minutes

Opening:

"ello, my name is Jake. I'm glad you all could join us here today. Let's get started with our hello song!"

Opening Song:
> **Good Morning** by Greg and Steve (We All Live Together Vol. 2 CD)

Discussion:
Today we're going to talk about playing sports. Sports are both fun and important. They are a form of physical fitness, which is good for your health. Some sports you play with a ball. Some sports you play with a bat. Some sports you play with a hoop. And some sports you just watch on TV. Today we're going to read some stories and sing some songs about games and sports. It's important to warm up your body and muscles before any sports so let's get warmed up.

Song Activity:
(Have children act out the song's lyrics.)
We Can Jump

> We can jump, jump, jump
> We can hop, hop, hop
> We can clap, clap, clap,
> We can stop, stop, stop,
> We can stretch up both our arms,
> We can reach and touch our toes,
> We can bend our knees a little bit,
> And sit down slow.

http://www.thebestkidsbooksite.com/funfingerplay.cfm?fingerplayid=348
http://www.thebestkidsbooksite.com/fingerplays-for-kids.cfm

Book Activity:
Froggy Plays Soccer by Jonathan London and Frank Remkiewicz. ISBN# 0140568093

Song Activity:
(Have children act out the song's lyrics.)
Shake My Sillies Out by Raffi (More Singable Songs CD)
http://www.metrolyrics.com/shake-my-sillies-out-lyrics-raffi.html

From *Storytimes for Children* by Stephanie G. Bauman. Santa Barbara, CA: Libraries Unlimited. Copyright © 2011.

Book Activity:
Mort the Sport by Robert Kraus and John Himmelman. ISBN# 0531302474

Song Activity:
(Have children act out the song's lyrics.)
Take Me out to the Ball Game
http://bussongs.com/songs/take_me_out_to_the_ball_game.php

Book Activity:
Take Me Out to the Ballgame by Jack Norworth and Alec Gillman. ISBN# 0689824335

Closing Song:
Goodbye by Francine Wheeler (Come Sit Beside Me CD)

Closing to Parents:
I have some books about games and sports on the table in the back of the room. Feel free to take them home with you today. If you need help finding some other books that you think you'll enjoy, please come talk to me. I hope you've had a good time today; and that you'll come see us again next week.

Additional Activity Ideas:

Skateboarding and Rollerblading

Set up an inside sport, such as dance revolution.

Explain how to get involved in sports locally and cheaply: community center/ youth center information.

This storytime is based closely on a storytime written by Jake Sexton.

Winter Animals

Anticipated Length: 45 Minutes

Opening:

 "**H**ello everyone. My name is Ashley. I am very glad that you came to join me at the library today. We are going to begin by singing a great Hello song, so everyone join in and give a great big wave hello to one another."

Opening Song:

Hello Everybody
http://www.peterandellen.com/lyrics/helloeverybody.mp3
(Depending on the size of the group you can then repeat the song substituting each child's name for the word "everybody" in the song.)

Discussion:

Its very cold outside today. There is a lot of ice and snow. In some parts of the world, the weather is like this all the time. Would you like to live in a place like that?

Activity:

Cold Weather Animals
Cut out pictures of various animals and hold them up to the children. We are going to try and figure out which animals live in places that are always cold, like the Arctic. Does a flamingo live in the arctic? How about a monkey? What about a penguin? Our first story is about a penguin that was a very odd bird.

Book Activity:

Tacky the Penguin by Helen Lester. ISBN# 0395562333

Song Activity:

(Have children act out the song's lyrics.)
The Snowkey Pokey

You put your right mitten in,
you take your right mitten out,
you put your right mitten in
and you shake it all about.
You do the snowkey pokey
and you turn yourself around.
That's what it's all about.
Additional verses:
You put your left mitten in . . .

From *Storytimes for Children* by Stephanie G. Bauman. Santa Barbara, CA: Libraries Unlimited.
Copyright © 2011.

> You put your right boot in . . .
> You put your left boot in . . .
> You put your hat in . . .
> You put your snowself in . . .

http://www.preschooleducation.com/swinter.shtml

Book Activity:
Animals in Winter by Henrietta Bancroft and Helen K. Davie. ISBN# 0064451658

Activity:
Mitten Match Up
Cut twelve mitten shapes from blank paper and make six pairs of identical mittens by drawing a pattern on them. Have the kids sit in a circle and take turns turning over two mittens to try to find a perfect pair. Game is over when all pairs have been uncovered.

Book Activity:
Someone Walks By: The Wonders of Winter Wildlife by Polly Carlson-Voiles. ISBN# 0980104564

Closing Song:
Goodbye Everybody
http://www.peterandellen.com/lyrics/helloeverybody.mp3
(Same tune as Hello Everybody song, but you say Goodbye and See you Soon.)

Closing to Parents:
We are all done for today! I hope to see you next week! To learn more about animals come check out all the books we have waiting for you!

This storytime is based closely on a storytime written by Ashley Sealy.

4

Smarties (7–8 Year Olds)

Who likes intelligent, inquisitive, interested children? We all do. How about 20–30 of them in your library for their weekly visit with you? Absolute sponges for random information, these Smarties, know a lot more than you might think, so please do not underestimate them! No more baby talk or over-annunciation if you are prone to it; these little Smarties would like you to speak to them with respect and listen to what they have to say. This is an absolutely crucial time to let your children and your students start to explore their interests and the world around them or they may become resentful of the restricted learning process and those invisible boundaries that well-meaning adults set up as cat's cradles around them.

If the children in the group are all interested in the nighttime sky or artwork, or really excited about hiking, it's time to start customizing those storytimes. These Smarties' world views are starting to expand just a bit, and they want to be a part of it, so let your storytimes reflect this. Recycling, saving animals, and future careers are on their minds. Reader theatre is much appreciated, as the students themselves get to act out stories, but are still at an age where this can be taken lightly, leaving room for goofiness and fun. If you have the same children each week, simple chapter stories would be well loved. This is a fun age to create storytimes because you never know what to expect, so keep on your toes, have lots of options, and be prepared for a great time!

Anatomy

Anticipated Length: 1 Hour

Opening:

"ello everyone and welcome to the library. Today we will be talking a bit about body parts. First I have a song that we can sing together about our parts."

Song Activity:
(Have children act out the song's lyrics.)
Dem Skeleton Bones
http://www.events-in-music.com/the-leg-bone-connected-to-the-knee-bone.html

Book Activity:
Parts by Ted Arnold. ISBN# 0140565337

Activity:
Body Parts Simon Says
Example:

> Simon Says:
> Touch your ear.
> Wiggle your toes.
> Bend your elbow,
> Shake your hands,
> Roll your shoulders.

Book Activity:
More Parts by Ted Arnold. ISBN# 0142501492

Song Activity:
(Have children act out the song's lyrics.)
Doctor, Doctor by Richard Graham
http://genkienglish.net/doctorsong.htm

Activity/Game:
Doctor Doctor Are You Ok?
http://genkienglish.net/doctor.htm
Here is an example of ESL students playing this game. It could be made more challenging for all your Smarties by using more difficult terms such as kneecap and cranium.
http://is.gd/5ruFN

Closing to Parents:
We had a great time learning about body parts. But guess what: animals and bugs and birds and fish all have different names for many of their body parts. I have put a ton of books out on the center table for any of you who would like to learn more about bodies! See you soon!

Additional Activity Ideas:

This storytime could be a more involved learning unit, especially for a school library. A skeleton will go over well, so bring one out if your school has one.

This storytime is based closely on a storytime written by Ashley Sealy.

 Notes

Birds

Anticipated Length: 1 Hour

Opening:

"Welcome to story time. Today we are going to be talking about birds! We will learn about some local birds, so you can find out which ones are flying around your neighborhood."

Book Activity:
Birds, Nests & Eggs by Mel Boring. ISBN# 155971624X

Activity:
Guest Speaker
Have a local bird rescue group come with a guest bird. Where I live there is a rescue called Hawk Watch that loves to give free talks to children about birds and bird safety. A guest speaker can instruct kids on what to do if they find a baby bird, or an injured bird.

Song Activity:
(Have children act out the song's lyrics.)
Way up in the Sky
http://www.thebestkidsbooksite.com/funfingerplay.cfm?fingerplayid=153
http://www.thebestkidsbooksite.com/fingerplays-for-kids.cfm

Book Activity:
Bird Calls by Frank Gallo. ISBN# 1584760648
This book is a guessing game for bird recognition with playable bird sounds and is perfect for storytime because the book might not survive general shelving/checkout.

Closing to Parents:
Thanks for coming today everyone! I hope you learned more about birds! We have many resources here in the library to learn more, I have set out a few on the back table. See you next week!

Additional Activity Ideas:

Learn more about local birds and identify them from the library windows.
Create paper airplane birds.
Show a video on birds.

From *Storytimes for Children* by Stephanie G. Bauman. Santa Barbara, CA: Libraries Unlimited. Copyright © 2011.

Bring a demo of what birds like to eat in bird feeders and when the best time of year is to feed them.

This storytime was written by Stephanie G. Bauman.

 Notes

Bugs

Anticipated Length: 1 Hour

Opening:

"Welcome to storytime today! Bugs are more than just creepy and crawly, many of them are really interesting and beautiful! They have important jobs to do and we can help them do their job by learning about them and understanding them better."

Book Activity:
Diary of a Worm by Doreen Cronin. ISBN# 006000150X
This is a fun and silly story told from the perspective of a little boy worm in diary form.

Activity:
Guest Bug Keeper
With the help of the local zoo or children's science museum or even pet shop, allow a guest speaker to talk about the creatures they bring. (Invite them to bring local species if possible so kids can learn about safety and respect for nature.) Even a dead bug collection will be of use for this activity.

Book Activity:
Everything Bug: What Kids Really Want to Know about Bugs by Cherie Winner. ISBN# 1559718919
A big, beautiful picture filled books with incredibly interesting information on bugs and insects.

Book Activity:
Bites and Stings by Alvin Silverstein, Virginia Silverstein, and Laura Silverstein Nunn. ISBN# 0531165590

Activity:
Egg Carton Bugs
Using various bits of egg carton, and various craft bits, the children can create fanciful bugs to take home. They can also put them in the yard and see if any bug makes them into a home.

Closing to Parents:
Thanks for coming today everyone! I hope you learned more about bugs and insects! The library has many resources to learn more, I have set a few out on the back table. See you next week!

Additional Activity Ideas:

Look at local bugs
Science lesson on a bug's role in the ecosystem
Camouflage and bugs

This storytime was written by Stephanie G. Bauman.

 Notes

Calendars

Anticipated Length: 1 Hour

Opening:

 "**W**elcome everyone! Today we are going to learn more about the months of the year and create our own calendar to take home."

Book Activity:
Selections from **Blue Monday** and **Friday the Thirteenth** by Lila Perl. ISBN# 0899193277
A great book full of trivia and reasoning behind the dates, days, and holidays on our calendars.

Rhyme Activity:
The Months Poem (30 Days Hath)
http://www.rhymes.org.uk/thirty_days_hath_september.htm
http://www.leapyearday.com/30Days.htm

Activity:
Part 1 of Create Your Own Calendar
Pass out the twelve blank month sheets, stapled at the top so they stay in order and are ready to be attached to the 11 by 17 backing sheet in part 2. Go through month by month adding holidays and birthdays with the children. Then give some free time to color in the names of the months.

Book Activity:
St. Patrick's Day: Parades, Shamrocks, and Leprechauns by Elaine Landau. ISBN# 076601777X
A detailed and fun book about St. Patrick's Day.
(You can use any book about a holiday. For example: Origins of Christmas, Mardi Gras, 4th of July).

Activity:
Part 2 of Create Your Own Calendar
On the top half a heavy piece of 11 by 17 paper, children can create a collage or even a single picture cut out of scrap magazines. On the bottom half, the calendar pages created in the first part of the activity can be attached by the librarian.

Closing to Parents:
I hope you had fun making your new calendar! Keeping track of the days is a fun way to know what's coming soon, like your birthday! These also make great gifts for your family! See you next week!

Additional Activity Ideas:

    History lesson on how the months and days got their names
    Cultural lesson on different types of calendars and date systems

This storytime was written by Stephanie G. Bauman.

Notes

Christmas Reader's Theatre

Anticipated Length: 40 Minutes

Opening:

 "**H**ello, my name is Jake. I'm glad you could join us today. Everybody stand up; let's start with our welcome song."

Song Activity:
(Have children act out the song's lyrics.)
Good Morning by Greg and Steve (We All Live Together Vol. 2 CD)

Discussion:
Today we are going to put on a play! Don't worry if you don't like to talk in front of everyone all by yourself, you can read along with someone else or you can be someone else in the theater! We will talk more about that in a minute!

Book Activity:
How Does the Show Go On: An Introduction to the Theater by Thomas Schumacher and Jeff Kurtti. ISBN# 1423100883

Activity:
Arthur's Christmas Reader's Theatre by Marc Brown.
http://www.timelessteacherstuff.com/readerstheater/ArthurChristmas.html
(This play is readily available online for free or little cost.)
Arthur's Christmas by Marc Brown. IBSN# 0316115363 (Book version)
This play has eight character parts and two narrators. If attendance is small, the librarian can read the leftover roles.

Discussion:
Talk about what the story meant. Make sure the children realize that the letter at the end was written by D. W. Ask the children why D. W. did what she did.

Activity:
Drawing
Have children:

1. Draw a picture of something that they would like for Christmas.
2. Draw a picture of something that they would give to Santa Claus for Christmas (like the characters in the story).
3. Draw a picture of the part they played, or a job they might like to have in the theatre.

From *Storytimes for Children* by Stephanie G. Bauman. Santa Barbara, CA: Libraries Unlimited. Copyright © 2011.

Closing to Parents:
Some books of plays that you can put on at home as well as some books on the theatre are ready for you on the back table. If you need help finding some other books that you think you'll enjoy, please come talk to me. I hope you've had a good time today, and that you'll come see us again next week.

Additional Activity Ideas:

> Once the children know the roles of the theatre, have them make their own play about Christmas.
> Have a speaker come from a local children's theatre group.
> Have a puppet theatre of the same play (children could even make lunch bag puppets for characters).

This storytime is based closely on a storytime written by Jake Sexton.

 Notes

Compare/Contrast

Anticipated Length: 40 Minutes

Opening:

"**H**ave children sit on carpet as they come in the library and sit down. Say: 'Criss-cross applesauce, hands in your lap. A, B, C, One, Two Three, Everybody's eyes on me.' "

Children Respond: "One, Two, eyes on you."

How many of you have heard the story *The Little Red Hen*? Today we are going to read two different versions of *The Little Red Hen*. The first one is the one you are probably most familiar with. The second one is just a little different.

Book Activity:
The Little Red Hen by Margot Zemach. ISBN# 0374445117

Discussion:
Our second version is a little different. Let's see if you can find some ways this story is different and some ways that it is the same.

Book Activity:
Armadilly Chili by Helen Ketteman. ISBN# 0807504572

Discussion:
Now boys and girls let's talk about how the stories are the same and how they are different. (Have something to write their responses on and post their answers.) Now boys and girls I want to read one more version of this story but this time you have to help me read. (Use an overhead and project the words for the students to read.) I will read the words in orange and you all read the words in pink. At the end there are words in blue and we all read those words together.

Book Activity:
You Read to Me, I'll Read to You: Very Short Fairy Tales to Read Together by Mary Ann Hoberman. ISBN# 0316146110
(Read *The Little Red Hen and the Grain of Wheat*, pp. 26–29)

Discussion:
Add any similarities and differences based on the addition of the last story. Which one was their favorite and why?

Closing to Parents:
I'm very glad you came today and I hope you enjoyed the stories. I look forward to seeing you next week. Enjoy your books and remember "Library books are like your shoes, you never come to school without your shoes, and you never come to school without your library books."

Additional Activity Ideas:

> Color a picture of a hen
> Talk about hens, roosters, and eggs
> Play a variation of the game Duck, Duck, Goose and call it something like Hen, Hen, Chicken.
> Discuss whether hens can fly or not.

This storytime is based closely on a storytime written by Elizabeth Turner.

 Notes

Crocodiles and Alligators

Anticipated Length: 40 Minutes

Opening:

 "**W**elcome to storytime. Today we are talking about the living dinosaurs and more!"

Activity:
Yoga Pose for Kids—Lion & Flamingo
http://www.lazylizardsyoga.com/poses.html
See others fun activities from:
Stories on the Move: Integrating Literature and Movement with Children, From Infants to Age 14 by Arlene Cohen. ISBN# 1591584183

Book Activity:
The Enormous Crocodile by Roald Dahl. ISBN# 0142414530

Book Activity:
All About Alligators by Jim Arnosky. ISBN# 0590467891

Discussion:
What is the difference between crocodiles and alligators? Do we have them around here? People in some countries have lived beside them for so many years that they have made stories and legends about them. Next I am going to read *Kanchil and the Crocodile: An Indonesian Folktale* to you. Then, we will split into groups and read our parts as a play. Each group will interpret and emphasize however they choose. That way we can see how different we all are when it comes to reading and our thoughts about it. No one can do it wrong, each telling will be right! We can even do it again another day if you want too!

Activity:
Kanchil and the Crocodile: A Play for Readers' Theater
From: *Multicultural Folktales for the Feltboard and Readers' Theater* by Judy Sierra. ISBN# 1573560030
(Before this storytime, have your felt board ready and make the patterns given in the book to use as you read the folktale. Have seven copies of the *Kanchil and the Crocodile: A Play for Readers' Theater* in folders for each character, the narrator, and yourself. See pages 3–10 of the book for recommendations for the felt board and how to do reader's theater.)

Activity:
Clothespin Alligator
http://www.busybeekidscrafts.com/Clothes-Pin-Alligator.html
Also see: Crafts for Kids Who Are Wild About Reptiles by Kathy Ross. ISBN# 0761303324

Closing to Parents:
Thanks for coming in today! Did you know the crocodiles and alligators are living dinosaurs. You will find books and materials on the back table about crocodiles and even some on dinosaurs.

Additional Activity Ideas:

Show children on a globe or online the places that alligators and crocodiles are naturally found.

Alligator skin craft from materials found outside, painted green.

See suggestions at this web site: http://www.thebestkidsbooksite.com/story details.cfm

This storytime is based closely on a storytime written by Kathy Burgener.

Food

Anticipated Length: 40 Minutes

Opening:

"Hello, my name is Jake, I'm glad you could join us today. Everybody, please stand up, and let's start with our welcome song."

Song Activity:
(Have children act out the song's lyrics.)
Good Morning by Greg and Steve (We All Live Together Vol. 2 CD)

Discussion:
Today we're going to talk about food. We have some fun stories about food, and a craft at the end that's about food too. And when we're done, you'll all be hungry enough to go home with mom or dad and eat some lunch.

Book Activity:
Cloudy with a Chance of Meatballs by Ron and Judi Barrett. ISBN# 0689707495

Book Activity:
Strega Nona by Tomie dePaola. ISBN# 0671666061

Book Activity:
The Biggest Sandwich Ever by Rita Gelman. ISBN# 059030559X

Activity:
Make a Menu
Materials: construction paper, glue sticks, scissors, food magazines, colored pens, and pencils. Children will cut pictures of foods out of the magazines and glue them on to the construction paper to make their own "menus." They should write the name of each dish underneath each picture. Menus can be one flat page, or folded in half like a menu at a restaurant.

Closing to Parents:
I have some books about food that you can make at home on the table in the back of the room; feel free to take them home with you today. If you need help finding some other books that you think you'll enjoy, please come talk to me. I hope you've had a good time today and that you'll come see us again next week.

From *Storytimes for Children* by Stephanie G. Bauman. Santa Barbara, CA: Libraries Unlimited. Copyright © 2011.

Additional Activity Ideas:

Invite a local chef/cook to talk about how their menus are chosen.

Learn about basic nutrition.

Learn how to make a simple recipe. (Even as simple as homemade claydough.)

Bring in some bizarre/exotic fruit and vegetables. (Get permission to give out samples.)

Have the children talk about their favorite and least favorite foods.

Color a pizza. Children can draw their favorite toppings.

This storytime is based closely on a storytime written by Jake Sexton.

 Notes

Geckos

Anticipated Length: 1 Hour

Opening:

 "**W**elcome to storytime. Today we are talking about geckos! We are also going to have a guest speaker!"

Activity:
Yoga Pose for Kids—**Lion and Lazy Lizard**
http://www.lazylizardsyoga.com/poses.html
See other fun activities from:
Stories on the Move: Integrating Literature and Movement with Children, From Infants to Age 14 by Arlene Cohen. ISBN# 1591584183

Discussion:
Today we are going to read a Balinese fairytale book titled *Go to Sleep Gecko!* by Margaret Read MacDonald. Does anyone know what the word Balinese means? It is the term used for the people who live on the island of Bali. Bali is an island of South Indonesia. Looking at the cover; do you think it looks scary or cute or funny? The drawing is how the illustrator, Geraldo Valerio thinks about geckos; it is not a real picture, just one of from his imagination (like a cartoon). What do you know about geckos?

Book Activity:
Go to Sleep Gecko! By Margaret Read MacDonald and Margaret Read. ISBN# 0874837804

Song Activity:
(Have children act out the song's lyrics.)
Gecko Song
http://www.buzzle.com/editorials/8-24-2006-106568.asp

Activity:
Guest Speaker
Invite a speaker from the Reptile Association, local zoo, or even reptile pet store to speak.
Licking Gecko Finger Puppet Craft
The gecko has no eyelids, so it must use its long tongue to keep its eyes moist.
From the book: **Crafts for Kids Who Are Wild About Reptiles** by Kathy Ross. ISBN# 0761303324

Closing to Parents:
Thanks for coming to storytime today! You will find lots of books about reptiles and their ancestors, dinosaurs, on the back table. See you next week!

Additional Activity Ideas:

Gecko coloring page: http://printables.kaboose.com/gecko.html
Gecko Web sites to view photos.
Hawaiian myths regarding geckos:
http://www.zimbio.com/Kauai+Hawaii/articles/67/Geckos+Our+Little+Guardians
http://www.coffeetimes.com/geckos.htm
http://www.to-hawaii.com/this-and-that.php

This storytime is based closely on a storytime written by Kathy Burgener.

 Notes

Going Batty

Anticipated Length: 1 Hour

Opening:

"Ask children come in to the library, ask them to please sit down on the carpet. 'Criss-cross applesauce, hands in your lap. A, B, C, One, Two Three, Everybody's eyes on me.'"

Children Respond: "One, Two, eyes on you."

Boys and girls, I have three really fun stories to share with you today. I call this the "Going Batty Storytime." All three stories have to do with Bats! You know some stories are nonfiction. That means they are true. Other stories are fiction. That means they are not true. They are pretend or made up stories. Our first story today is nonfiction. The title of the book is *Big Brown Bat*. The author is Rick Chrustowski. The illustrator is also Rick Chrustowski! I think it is pretty amazing that he wrote the words and drew the pictures for this book. The best thing about this book is it doesn't read like nonfiction. Sometimes nonfiction books are just fact, after fact, after fact. That gets kind of boring sometimes, but this book reads like a story with a beginning a middle and an end. So if you are ready show me my good listeners.

Book Activity:
Big Brown Bat by Rick Chrustowski. ISBN# 0805074996

Discussion:
That was a fun nonfiction book. Who can tell me something we learned about bats from this book. (Allow time for discussion.) Our next book is a fiction book about bats. The title is *Stellaluna*. The author is Janell Cannon and she is also the illustrator. The pictures in this book are beautiful and to make it easier for you to see the pictures I am going to read the "Big Book" edition, but we have the regular size book for you to check out. (Place book on easel and read.)

Book Activity:
Stellaluna by Janell Cannon. ISBN# 015201540X

Discussion:
Did you like that story? I really like the pictures. I said the story was fiction, but there are some facts about bats in the story. Do bats talk? (No!) When are bats awake during the night or during the day? (Night) What do bats eat? How do bats sleep? All of these are facts about bats, so even though the story is fiction, it still has some nonfiction information. If you are ready for our third and final book, show me my good listeners. (Read the book.)

Book Activity:
Bats at the Library by Brian Lies. ISBN# 061899923X

Closing to Parents:
Now, I want you to tell me if that book was nonfiction or fiction? (Wait for response.) Yes, you are right. That book was fiction. Can bats read? (Wait for response.) No! Bats cannot read, but you can! So I hope you enjoyed our stories today about bats. I hope you enjoy the books you choose, and I look forward to seeing you next week. Oh, one more thing, we learned that bats are not blind, but they do fly around at night when it is dark, so instead of depending on their eyes to see where they are going they use sonar to hear where they are going. In order for bats not to run into things and to locate their food, they have to be very good listeners. So I want to "listen like a bat" to your teacher and she will tell you what to do next.

Additional Activity Ideas:

Have a local animal control officer come to talk about bat safety.
Play an audio sequence of bat noises online and talk about echolocation.
Show a short documentary about bats.

This storytime is based closely on a storytime written by Elizabeth Turner.

Kites

Anticipated Length: 40 Minutes

Opening:

"**H**ello and welcome to our storytime about kites! We're glad you came to visit the library. Today, we will be talking and reading about kites and how to make them. You can even make one to take home!"

Discussion:

Give a brief history of kites and their uses from sources at your library or internet options.

> http://en.wikipedia.org/wiki/Kite
>
> http://www.gombergkites.com/nkm/hist1.html
>
> http://www.kitehistory.com/
>
> http://www.nationalkitemonth.org/history/

Book Activity:

Let's Fly a Kite by Stuart Murphy. ISBN# 0739843826

Book Talk:

The Kite Fighters by Linda Sue Park. ISBN# 0440418135

This story, set in Seoul, South Korea in 1473, is about Young-sup and his brother Kee-sup. The New Year's kite-fighting contest is coming up and they are getting their kites ready. Each brother is talented in a different way. Kee-sup, the oldest, is very good at designing and building kites and Young-sup is very good at flying kites and keeping them under control. Young-sup knows that he must help his older brother win the contest, as is the tradition, but he still hopes that he will be able to shine in the contest. This story talks about kites and their role in the culture of Korea as well as the two brothers and how they learn to work together. It is an excellent book and I'm sure you would like to take it home to read.

Kites for Everyone: How to make and Fly Them by Margaret Greger. ISBN# 0486452956

This is an excellent book that has over 50 designs and instructions on how to make kites, wind socks, and parachutes. It is full of great pictures and the instructions are clearly written with drawings to help you when you are making a kite or other project. The designs range from very simple to complex and this book is a good one for all ages of kite makers!

Song Activity:
(Have children act out the song's lyrics.)
Let's Go Fly a Kite
http://bussongs.com/songs/lets_go_fly_a_kite.php

Activity:
Make a Kite
http://kids.nationalgeographic.com/Activities/Crafts/Kite-craft

Closing to Parents:
Thanks so much for coming to our storytime about kites! We hope you had fun and that you will remember to browse our craft section. It's in the 745s. You can find other books that you might like about other craft projects. The library has several books about kite-making and stories about kites as well. In fact, the library has many books about how to make and do things. You just have to think about what you're interested in and we can help you find a book about it!

Additional Activity Ideas:

> Discuss kite safety.
> Explain how to buy a kite that's right for you.
> Describe modern-day adaptations of kites, such as wind surfing.

This storytime is based closely on a storytime written by Julie Andrews-Jotham.

Life Cycles

Anticipated Length: 40 Minutes

Opening:

"**A**sk children to please sit down on the carpet as they come in to the library."

"Criss-cross applesauce, hands in your lap. A, B, C, One, Two Three, Everybody's eyes on me."

Children Respond: "One, Two, eyes on you." Boys and girls, your teacher tells me you have been studying life cycles. Our stories today are about life cycles. Two of our stories are nonfiction. That means they are true. One of our stories is fiction that means it is made up. Our first story today is about frogs and it is nonfiction. It talks about the life cycle of the frog. The author is Alex Vern. He wrote the words.

Book Activity:
Where Do Frogs Come From? By Alex Vern. ISBN# 0152048847

Discussion:
Boys and girls, at the end of the story it told us what frogs eat. Who can tell me what frogs eat? That's right, they eat bugs. I want you to remember that because it is going to be important when we read our last story. Our next story is about the life cycle of butterflies. The author is Joanne Ryder and the illustrator is Lynne Cherry. I love the illustrations in this book.

Book Activity:
Where Butterflies Grow by Joanne Ryder. ISBN# 0140558586

Discussion:
Those books are very interesting and I'm sure you learned a lot about butterflies and frogs. Now I have book to share with you that is fiction. That means the story is made up. It has a very surprising ending.

Book Activity:
Tadpole's Promise by Jeanne Willis. ISBN# 0689865244

Discussion:
Oh my! What happened? The frog ate his true love! Did that surprise you? It shouldn't have if you were paying attention. Remember what do frogs eat? That's right, insects, or bugs. What is a butterfly? That's right, an insect. So you should have known that relationship could never work out. It was doomed from the beginning.

Closing to Parents:
That's all we have time for today. I hoped you learned a lot about life cycles. I hope you enjoy your books and I will see you next week. Remember, what do I always say? "Books are like your shoes. You never come to school without your shoes, and you never come to school without your library books."

Additional Activity Ideas:

Borrow a science display on the life cycle of a butterfly.
Have a guest come from a local pet store with a frog.
Discuss if humans have a life cycle.
Color a life cycle chart.

This storytime is based closely on a storytime written by Elizabeth Turner.

Hairy Situations

Anticipated Length: 1 Hour

Opening:

"Ask children to please sit on carpet as they come into the library. 'Criss-cross applesauce, hands in your lap. A, B, C, One, Two Three, Everybody's eyes on me.'"

Children Respond: "One, Two, eyes on you." Boys and girls I have three really fun stories to share with you today. I call this the Hairy Situation storytime. All three stories have to do with hair!

Book Activity:
Stephanie's Ponytail by Robert Munsch. ISBN# 1550374850

Discussion:
Boys and girls, what lesson did you learn from this story? (Don't be a copycat or you might end up bald!) What do you think about copycats? Is it being a copycat when you see someone's idea and think you can make it better? (That's called being inspired.) How can you give someone credit? (Mention their name).

Book Activity:
Big Bushy Mustache by Gary Soto. ISBN# 06998030X

Discussion:
That was a fun story. I like that some of it was English and some of it was Spanish. I bet next time the teacher tells him to do something he follows directions! Have you ever had a "bad hair day?" You know, one of those days when you can't get your hair to cooperate. Well you have never had a bad hair day quite like the boy in our next story.

Book Activity:
Aaron's Hair by Robert Munsch. ISBN# 0439192587

Activity:
Make a Head with Hair Craft
Have the students put hair on an outline of a head. Have an outline of a head on paper. Give the students crayons to draw their face. Then have yarn in various colors so they can glue hair or a mustache on their picture. Have all the materials on the tables ready before storytime. You will need several bottles of glue, the outline of the heads, one per child, yarn in several colors pre-cut to various lengths, crayons, and extra yarn, uncut.

Closing to Parents:

"A, B, C, One, Two, Three, all eyes on me." Students respond, "One, Two, eyes on you." I want to thank you for coming this week. Have a good week and I will see you at our next storytime.

Additional Activity Ideas:

Do a slide show of hairstyles from other countries.

Martial artists and police must keep their hair short . . . why?

Fun facts about hair, including hair growth after death, nose hair, reasons for body hair, and reasons for hair colors.

This storytime is based closely on a storytime written by Elizabeth Turner.

Notes

Library Etiquette

Anticipated Length: 1 Hour

Opening:

"Ask children to please sit on carpet as they come into the library. 'Criss-cross applesauce, hands in your lap. A, B, C, One, Two Three, Everybody's eyes on me.'"

Children Respond: "One, Two, eyes on you." (This works because most are returning students.)

My name is Mrs. Turner. I am the librarian. I remember some of you from last year, but there are some new faces. This is our library and today we are going to go over the rules for the library. I have some books today that talk about library rules.

Book Activity:
Library Lion by Michelle Knudsen. ISBN# 0763622621

Discussion:
The author was inspired to write this book because of the statues of lions in front of the library in New York City." (Show picture of the lions in front of the New York Public Library Central Branch downloaded from the Internet.) What rule did the lion need to know? (Wait for response.) That's right, 'The library is a quiet place.' Our next story talks about some of the other rules in the library. I have a special friend to help me with this story. (Show Shelf Elf and Bookapillar purchased from Upstart.) Who is ready for our next story? Show me my good listeners. That's right good listeners are sitting criss-cross applesauce with your hands in your lap. The author of this story is Jackie Mims Hopkins. She wrote the words and Rebecca Thornburgh is the illustrator. That means she drew the pictures.

Book Activity:
Shelf Elf by Jackie Mims Hopkins. IBSN# 1932146164

Discussion:
Our next book is a book of poetry about the library. We are not going to read all the poems, just a few. The author or poet, since the book is poetry, is Patrick Lewis. The illustrator is Kyle Stone." (Read a few of the poems as time and attention allow.)

Book Activity:
Please Bury Me in the Library by Patrick J Lewis. ISBN# 0152163875

From *Storytimes for Children* by Stephanie G. Bauman. Santa Barbara, CA: Libraries Unlimited. Copyright © 2011.

Activity Ideas:
Treasure Hunt
A test for you as well as the students is to find out how much they know about the library. Prizes can be book marks, buttons, or extra copies of books.

Closing to Parents:
"A, B, C, One, Two, Three, all eyes on me." Students respond, "One, Two, eyes on you." I want to thank you for coming this week. Have a good week and I will see you next week.

Additional Activity Ideas:

This storytime could be woven into a much larger library introduction or refresher unit.

This Storytime is based closely on a storytime written by Elizabeth Turner.

 Notes

Magical Creatures

Anticipated Length: 1 Hour

Opening:

"Welcome to storytime. Today we are going to be talking about magical creatures. You may have heard of dragons and unicorns, but today we are going to talk about many other kinds you may not have heard about."

Book Activity:

The Book of Dragons & Other Mythical Beasts by Joe Nigg. ISBN# 0764155105
This book is a collection of mythical beasts with stunning illustrations. It is large and easily viewed by a storytime group.

Activity:

Guess the Creature
Starting with a small piece, like a horn, show students a cutout from a mythical creature. The librarian describes the part. For example, "this creature has hooves."
Continue this exercise including some creatures that were not talked about in the book for instance creatures from Harry Potter, and other popular movies.

Book Activity:

Selections from **Here there be Unicorns** by Jane Yolen. ISBN# 0152099026
This book is a collection of short stories, poems, and folklore about unicorns. There is also a similar book by the same author about dragons, witches, and ghosts.

Activity:

Create Your Own Mythical Creature
Using whatever craft supplies are at hand (including sticks, leaves, and twigs for those children who want to create elf-like creatures) the children can draw, glue, color, and create their own imagined creature. They will need to be able to tell the class about their creation, answering questions such as what it can do, how it does this (with wings? claws? magic), where it lives, what it eats, if it can speak, etc.

Closing to Parents:

Thanks for coming today everyone! I hope you learned more about magical creatures! The library has many resources to help you learn more, I have set a few out on the back table. See you next week!

Additional Activity Ideas:

Use a history of mythical creatures for a history and symbolism lesson.
Show clips from a Harry Potter movie to show some mythical creatures (unicorns, gryphons).

This storytime was written by Stephanie G. Bauman.

 Notes

Mardi Gras

Anticipated Length: 1 Hour

Opening:

"Welcome to storytime! Today we are going to talk about a holiday that you might have heard about it. It is a mix between a cultural celebration, a religious holiday, and mostly a giant party. It happens each year in New Orleans, Louisiana. (Show on globe or map.) We are going to read some books on Mardi Gras then have our own celebration."

Book Activity:
Mardi Gras: A Cajun Country Celebration by Diane Hoyt-Goldsmith. ISBN# 0823411842
Interesting accurate information from the point of view of a young fiddler.

Activity:
Create a Mardi Gras Mask
The children will create a colorful mask from a mask template pre-printed on heavy paper. They can decorate it any way they like. Then, using tape or staples, attach heavy straws or chopsticks as a handle.

Book Activity:
Mimi's First Mardi Gras by Alice Couvillon and Elizabeth Moore. ISBN# 088289840X
This book shows a more traditional view of a New Orleans Mardi Gras. It's fun and colorful.

Mardi Gras Conga
With Cajun music playing children can bend under the limbo pole and parade around the children's portion of the library in a conga line wearing their new masks.

Closing to Parents:
Thanks for coming today everyone! I hope you learned more about Mardi Gras! We have many resources here in the library to learn more, I have set a few out on the back table. See you next week!

Additional Activity Ideas:

> Learn more about local state holidays.
> Watch a video on Mardi Gras.
> Talk about why Cajun is an important culture aspect of the United States and explain its history.

This storytime was written by Stephanie G. Bauman.

From *Storytimes for Children* by Stephanie G. Bauman. Santa Barbara, CA: Libraries Unlimited. Copyright © 2011.

Multi-Cultural Festivals

Anticipated Length: 1 Hour

Opening:

"**H**ello everyone. My name is Ashley. Today we are going to be talking about multicultural festivals, these are holidays that are celebrated around the world. Today we will be talking about Christmas, Hanukkah, Diwali, and Kwanzaa."

Discussion:
Christmas is on December 25 in the United States each year. Christmas commemorates the birth of Jesus Christ. Santa Claus has become a part of this holiday and we have other legends and traditions.

Book Activity:
Christmas (Rookie Read-About Holidays) by David F. Marx. ISBN# 0516271539. (Read Selections)
Humphrey's First Christmas by Carol Heyer. ISBN# 0824955595
Saint Nicholas: The Real Story of the Christmas Legend by Julie Stiegemeyer. ISBN# 0758613415

Discussion:
Hanukkah is an eight-day Jewish holiday commemorating the rededication of the Holy Temple in Jerusalem at the time of the Maccabean Revolt of the second century BCE. The festival is observed by the kindling of the lights of a special candelabrum, the nine-branched *Menorah* or *Hanukah*, one light on each night of the holiday, progressing to eight on the final night.

Book Activity:
The Menorah Story by Mark Podwal. ISBN# 0688157580

Discussion:
Diwali is a significant festival in Hinduism, Sikhism, Buddhism, and Jainism, and an official holiday in India. Diwali is known as the *Festival of Lights*. They light divas, cotton-like string wicks inserted in small clay pots filled with coconut oil, to signify victory of good over the evil within an individual. The five-day festival of Diwali occurs on the new moon between October 13 and November 14.

Book Activity:
Holidays Around the World: Celebrate Diwali by Deborah Heiligman. ISBN# 1426302916

Discussion:

Kwanzaa is a week-long African American holiday honoring African heritage. Participants light a kinara (candle holder). Kwanzaa consists of seven days of celebration, featuring activities such as candle lighting and ends in a feast and gift giving. It was created by Ron Karenga and was first celebrated from December 26, 1966 to January 1, 1967.

Book Activity:

My First Kwanzaa by Karen Katz. ISBN# 080507077X

Book Activity:

Multi-Cultural Festivals Memory Game
Print double images of various festival-related images on cardstock. Cut them out for a matching game.

Closing to Parents:

I hope you enjoyed learning about multicultural festivals. I have some books if you would like to learn more. Thank you for joining me today!

This storytime is based closely on a storytime written by Ashley Sealy.

Robert Munsch—Creative Storytelling

Anticipated Length: 40 Minutes

Opening:

"Hello everyone, my name is Ashley. I am very glad that you came to join me at the library today because we are going to talk a bit about one of my favorite authors and storytellers, Robert Munsch. Has anyone ever heard of Robert Munsch before? Have you heard or read any of his stories? Did you enjoy them?"

Robert Munsch

Robert Munsch is a Canadian author who has published over 55 books. The really neat thing about Robert Munsch is that he has the ability to tell really hilarious stories right off the top of his head. In fact, in most cases he tells stories to groups of children like you. He keeps telling and retelling the stories until they seem just right and then he writes them down and has them published. He even uses many of the children that he meets in his stories. We are going to begin by reading one of my favorite Robert Munsch books together.

Book Activity:
Thomas' Snowsuit by Robert Munsch. ISBN# 0920303323

Discussion:
Did you like that story? Did you know that many stories follow a pattern? A story usually has three very important parts: Introduction or Beginning which introduces characters and setting, Middle which introduces a problem, and End which resolves the problem. Can you identify these three parts from the Thomas' Snowsuit story?

Does anyone know what the word "setting" means? (The setting is where the story takes place.) What was the setting of the story we just read together? Who were the characters in the story? Who was the main character? How do you know that? Now we will listen to Robert Munsch telling a story to a group of children just like you. If you like you can close your eyes and imagine what the story would look like. Notice how Robert Munsch gets the children to make noises to help tell the story.

Activity:
Murmel, Murmel Munsch by Robert Munsch. ISBN# 1897166273

There are a number of available audio books, where Robert Munsch reads to a live audience. Also, sound clips of him reading stories in their entirety are available at: http://www.robertmunsch.com/

Discussion:
What was the setting of that story? Who were the characters? Was there a main character? What happened at the beginning? Was there a problem? How was it solved?

Activity:
Create a story as a group.
(*Children sit in a circle and take turns telling parts of a story.*)
I'll start. We can make this story silly, scary, or maybe mysterious. Let's try to make sure our story has a good beginning, middle, and end. (A story can be limited to one sentence or even one word.)
"One day, I was walking to the library when I saw the strangest thing . . . "
Continue until everyone has had a turn and/or the story is complete.

Closing to Parents:
Thank you for coming to visit me at the library. I hope you enjoyed learning about Robert Munsch and storytelling. I hope that you will continue to create interesting stories of your own. If you write a good story, maybe you could bring it to the library and share it with me. I would love to read it. I have displayed some more Robert Munsch books, in case you would like to take some home. Have a great day!

This storytime is based closely on a storytime written by Ashley Sealey.

Shel Silverstein

Anticipated Length: 40 Minutes

Opening:

"Hi everyone! Welcome to storytime. Today we are going to be talking about a famous poet named Shel Silverstein and learning more about poetry. Let's get started."

Opening Activity:
Fast and Silly Direction Game
This game can be played in multiple rounds. Starting with the librarian (as a demonstration), a variety of direction is given for the children to act on. For example "sit, stand, turn right, turn left, eyes closed, pat head." The faster these calls are given the better. If someone messes up they are out. This is a fairly quiet game except for the laughing!

Book Activity:
Falling Up by Shel Silverstein. ISBN# 0060248025. Selected Poems
Who wants a cheap Rhinoceros? by Shel Silverstein. ISBN# 1416996133. Selections.
A Giraffe and a Half by Shel Silverstein. ISBN# 0060256559. Selections.

Activity:
Creating a Visual Representation of Written Material
The children choose a poem or story by Shel Silverstein and make a picture about it by drawing, cutting and gluing pieces of different colored paper, being creative to make your interpretation or image of what you see when you hear or read Silverstein's books. Variations can include each child taking a line of the poem to do this activity. They can then line up and each read their line as they hold up their creation.

Closing to Parents:
Thanks for coming today! I hope you enjoyed the poetry and had a great time. Shel Silverstein has written several books if you want to read more. Also I have more books from different poets and how to create your own poetry!

Additional Activity Ideas:

Pizza, Pigs, and Poetry: How to Write a Poem by Jack Prelutsky. ISBN# 0061434485
Limericks and tongue twisters are always a hit!

This storytime is based closely on a storytime written by Melissa Castagna.

Treasure and Map Making

Anticipated Length: 1 Hour

Opening:

"Welcome to storytime! Today we are going to talk about treasures and map making. Understanding where you are and using maps can come in handy someday for more than finding buried treasure. When you know how to use a map you can travel the world!"

Book Activity:
Buried Treasure, a Pirate's Tale by Carroll Harrison Kehne. ISBN# 0870336010
This is a story about historical pirates, their haunts, and their treasures.

Activity:
Create a Map
The children will draw a map of the children's area of the library, with colors and basic labels.

Song Activity:
The Pirate Song
http://www.themeunits.com/Pirates_song.html

Book Activity:
Selections from **True-Life Treasure Hunts** by Judy Donnelly. ISBN# 0679839801
(This book is a collection of various real-life treasure hunts from pirates to ships to trainwrecks.)

Activity:
Find the Treasure
Using various clues, create a scavenger hunt in the library. For instance clues like, "where you go to find the book you are looking for" or "where you go if you are thirsty?" Encourage children to look at their map before racing off. The final prize can be neat bookmarks, or reading posters, whatever you have a lot of to give out as prizes (but no food!).

Closing to Parents:
Thanks for coming today everyone! I hope you learned more about map making and treasure! There are a ton of resources here in the library to learn more, I have set a few out on the back table. See you next week!

From *Storytimes for Children* by Stephanie G. Bauman. Santa Barbara, CA: Libraries Unlimited. Copyright © 2011.

Additional Activity Ideas:

Geocaching with a GPS unit on the grounds and nearby—an amazing treasure hunt activity.

Tie this lesson to a lesson on archeology.

Learn more about pirate history.

Learn more about modern-day pirates.

Learn more about compasses and maps.

This storytime was written by Stephanie G. Bauman.

Notes

5

Old Souls (9–10 Year Olds)

These bright children are already pretty worldly, and it's a scary world out there. Creating storytimes that enable these Old Souls to feel empowered is a gift. This is an excellent time for "how to" books and correlating activities. For example, reading about gardening, then creating a baby food jar garden is a way for these children to use available material to evoke change. This also provides a great opportunity for interesting guest speakers such as archeologists, artists, bee keepers, and video game designers.

Old Souls want to explore the world around them but might feel a bit caged by both their age and by traditional education (e.g., why can't we learn about the Space Program instead of history)? By teaching them the skills to find information on their own and allowing them to take charge of their own learning, they can take back a bit of control and learn how to accomplish finding out more about what they are actually interested in. For you, this means leaving a lot of time at the end of each storytime for questions and answers and reference direction. Each storytime should inspire and serve as a jumping off point that allows the children to see what a wonderful world of resources is available to them, no matter their age and say in their formal education. Longer activities such as researching, writing, and acting out plays can be a fun and engaging way for these Old Souls to find knowledge and put it to action. This is also a perfect time for book talks both fiction and nonfiction. For this, you pick out books and materials they might have missed or might like, such as new fiction books or a cluster of fiction books in a certain genre, the history of skateboarding, or how to use a computer program to make music, and then you give an intriguing summary and read a snippet. This is a great way to promote the library and its materials.

Old Souls will consider they have outgrown storytime at the public library, so most of these consider classroom applications in addition to activities in the school library. Public and school librarians share in the responsibility for continuing to create a focus on lifelong learning within their children.

Adventure Stories (Booktalk)

Anticipated Length: 30 Minutes

Opening:

"Good morning! Today I am going to share with you my favorite type of story, adventure stories."

Booktalks:

1. **Hatchet** by Gary Paulsen. ISBN# 0027701301.

   This is a typical adventure novel. The main character is a boy who ends up in the wilderness and has to learn how to survive. It is part of a series of books, so if you like this one, you will probably like the others in the series too. The book is, *Hatchet*, by Gary Paulsen. The main character is Brian. His parents are divorced and he is going to stay with his father for the summer. He has to travel on a small plane. Unfortunately, the pilot dies and the plane crashes. Brian is left alone. He has to learn to build a fire, a shelter, fish, hunt, and defend himself from all kinds of dangers. One of the most surprisingly difficult things he has to deal with is mosquitoes. You wouldn't think mosquitoes could be such a bother, but Brian is plagued by them almost constantly.

2. **Touching Spirit Bear** by Ben Mikaelsen. ISBN# 0060291494.

   Our second story is also a typical adventure story. The title of the book is, *Touching Spirit Bear*, by Ben Mikaelsen. The main character, Cole, is a boy who gets in trouble all the time. His parents have always given him everything he wants, but he is still very angry, and he is a bully. One day his anger comes to a head and he beats up a another boy. The boy almost dies and Cole is in bigger trouble than he has ever been in his life. His parents can do nothing to save him this time. He's going to juvenile hall and that's the end of that, or maybe not.

   A parole officer who happens to be Native American is assigned to Cole's case. The parole officer thinks he has better idea about how to help Cole. They send Cole to an island where he has to live alone. He has everything he needs to survive, but no frills. He has a cabin, and food, so compared to Brian in our first story he has it made. But Cole's anger gets the best of him again and he sets fire to his cabin with all the supplies inside. So now he is in a desperate situation, but he still blames everyone else for his problems. That is when he sees a bear. In his anger, he does possibly the dumbest thing anyone has ever done, he attacks the bear, by throwing rocks at it. Well, you can imagine who won that fight. Now Cole is alone, injured, and almost dead. How is he going to survive? Will he survive? Will he finally figure out that he is the reason for his problems and no one else?

3. **The Maze of Bones** by Rick Riordan. ISBN# 9780545090544

The third adventure story I am going to share with you is also part of a series, *The 39 Clues*. One unusual thing about this series is that each book in the series will be written by a different author. The series is multimedia formatted. That means you can read the printed book and also learn more on the Web site.

The first book in the series is, *The Maze of Bones*, by Rick Riordan. Amy and a boy, Dan, are the two main characters in the story. Have any of you ever watched, *The Amazing Race*? This story is a little like that.

Amy and Dan go to the funeral of their grandmother. There they learn that their family is the most powerful, wealthiest family that ever lived. They learn that they have some very important ancestors. Their grandmother had a very tricky will to determine who would inherit all the family wealth. The person that solves the mystery of the 39 clues first, will inherit everything. This causes turmoil among the family as each individual family travels all over the world trying to find the answers. There is plenty of action in this book, lots of explosions, secret passages, and mysterious strangers.

Closing to Parents:

So if action and adventure are for you, these books will be fun. The library has many other adventure books, but they are not all together on a single shelf. These books are fiction and fiction books are arranged in alphabetical order by the author's last name. I know that not everyone likes adventure books, but I hope I was able to show some of you some books another time that you might find more interesting. Who knows? If you try one adventure story, you might find out you do like adventure stories after all.

This storytime is based on a storytime written by Elizabeth Turner.

Clothing Design

Anticipated Length: 45 Minutes

Opening:

"Welcome. Thanks for coming in today. Today, we are going to talk a little about clothing design. What you wear does not have to be dictated by what anyone else wears, not movie stars or your classmates. You don't need to wear the newest fad or the most expensive pair of jeans. Thrift shopping and creating your own designs and alterations can be much better and a lot less expensive. Do you need to learn how to use a sewing machine? That would be helpful, but glue, tape, and a needle and thread are even better!"

Book Activity:

Generation T: 108 Ways to Transform a T-Shirt by Megan Nicolay. ISBN# 0761137858

This book can serve as a template for discussion. Are these t-shirts in style? What ideas does it give the student?. What questions does it bring up that they can research? Like what kind of glue holds up for washing?

Book Activity:

Low-Sew Boutique: 25 Quick & Clever Projects Using Ready-Mades by Cheryl Weiderspahn. ISBN# 0896894347

This book uses household items to create fun projects. What ideas does this book bring up? What can you do with unused school junk? Last year's school lost and found might bring up some fun project ideas.

Book Activity:

Born-Again Vintage: 25 Ways to Deconstruct, Reinvent, and Recycle Your Wardrobe by Bridgett Artise and Jen Karetnick. ISBN# 0307405273

This great book provides a neat jumping off point for what to do with your old clothes. Brainstorm and discuss the possibilities.

Activity:

MP3 Player Holder

http://kids.nationalgeographic.com/Activities/Crafts/Mp3-player

Additional Activity Ideas:

Have a copy of the magazine *Readymade* to look at. It has amazing "do it yourself with only a few items" type projects.

Have locations of sewing classes ready.

Explore fashion magazines for ideas. How to stay ahead of the "trends"? Make your own!

Where local designers sell their clothes.

Have a fashion designer come speak. They are usually found at non-mall, off the beaten path stores.

If there are a lot of boys in the group, you can do scarf designs, belt make-overs, and wallet re-do's.

This storytime is based on an activity suggested by Josh Mitchell.

 Notes

Comic Book Fun

Anticipated Length: 45 Minutes

Opening:

"Thanks for coming today! (Hold up a comic book or anime book.) Have you ever seen a book that looks like this? What is it called? That's right, it is a comic book."

Discussion:

What makes a comic book different than a normal chapter book?

What are some popular comics that you know?

Who are some popular characters?

What comic book characters have been made into films?

Activity:

Sequencing Activity

Cut comic strips out of the newspaper and cut out the individual squares. Separate the class into small groups and have them put the squares in the correct sequence.

Book Activity:

Comic Books and Manga by Eddie Robson. ISBN# 0778738353. Selections

Activity:

Crazy Captioning

Print out some funny pictures. Have the children fill out clever captions to the pictures using speech balloons. Share the pictures with everyone afterwards for a good laugh. National Geographic Kids have great examples of this at: http://kids.nationalgeographic .com/Activities/Cartoons/Cartoonpenguinpastimes?vgnextfmt=alternate

Comic Character Crossword (See if you or the children can say this five times quickly!) Using an online crossword generator, create a crossword puzzle using the names of popular comic book characters.

Example: http://www.puzzle-maker.com/CW/

Closing to Parents:

I have put some comic books on the table so that you can borrow them with your library card if you wish. If you have any comic characters that you like but you don't see them here, let me know and I will see what I can find for you. Thank you for joining me today.

Additional Activity Ideas:

Booktalks on the comics you have in house.

Have a local comic book store owner come in to talk about their favorites and about collecting.

Show an anime movie, even episodes of Pokemon are great!

This storytime is based closely on a storytime written by Ashley Sealey.

Notes

Cowboys/Girls

Anticipated Length: 45 Minutes

Opening:

"Today we are talking about the old west and the cowboys and girls who lived there!"

Book Activity:
Eyewitness: Cowboy by David S Murdoch. ISBN# 0789458543
Eyewitness: Wild West by Stuart Murray. ISBN# 0756610974
Selected Passages.

Activity:
Playing Horseshoes
Play an indoor version of this game using Styrofoam or heavy cardboard (can be made from old packing material cut up). Outdoor sets can be purchased inexpensively online (such as from Amazon).

Booktalks on Cowboy Books:
(Read selected text passages)

1. **My Name Is America: The Journal of Joshua Loper, a Black Cowboy**
   By Walter Dean Myers. ISBN# 0590026917
      Being a cattle drive cowboy is tough enough, but being young and African American presents extra challenges for this great main character.
2. **In the Days of the Vaqueros: America's First True Cowboys** by Russell Freedman. ISBN# 0395967880
      The story of the vaqueros, the first cow herders in the west, is told in this inform-ative and interesting book that includes historic photographs.
3. **Born to Be a Cowgirl: A Spirited Ride through the Old West** by Candace C. Savage. ISBN# 1582460191
      This story of women in the west includes journal excerpts and photographs.

Activity:
The Legend of Lightning Larry by Aaron Shepard
http://bms.westport.k12.ct.us/mccormick/rt/rtscripts/lightning_larry.htm
To produce this play, the librarian will help children choose their roles and act as the "director" during rehearsal. The program will culminate with the children performing for parents and other library-goers. The actual performance will last approximately 10 minutes.

Closing to Parents:
Thanks for coming today! This library is full of information on cowboys, the old west, and even information on ranching, horseback riding, and Native Americans, so it's time to get started reading! See everyone next time!

Additional Activity Ideas:

Presentations on Ghost Towns

Craft of painting their own bandanas

Create wanted posters

Learn cowboy campfire songs.

Have games and prizes such as sheriffs' badges, fake mustaches and plastic harmonicas.

Have a guest horse owner come and talk about caring for a horse

Read up and present on any local cowboy history.

This storytime is based closely on a storytime written by Josh Mitchell.

Environment and Recycling

Anticipated Length: 45 Minutes

Opening:

"Hey everyone, glad to see you! Today we are going to talk about the environment and recycling. Do any of you recycle at home? What is recyclable? We are going to also talk about reusing."

Book Activity:
A Hot Planet Needs Cool Kids: Understanding Climate Change and What You Can Do about It by Julie Hall. ISBN# 0615155855
(Read selections about how children can help at home.)

Activity:
Empty the Garbage
Explain what recycling in the library does. Take a rather full garbage can (office type not bathroom) and empty it over a plastic bag on a table. Talk about what is recyclable and how much of the garbage didn't need to go in the can. Kids will love the blatant grossness of this activity as they see chewed gum and old food.

Book Activity:
How We Know What We Know about Our Changing Climate: Scientists and Kids Explore Global Warming by Lynne Cherry. ISBN# 1584691034
Everything about climate change explained simply without the scare tactics that panic kids.

Discussion:
Not everything can be recycled, but can it be reused? What about composted?

Activity:
Fun with Phonebooks
Re-use your phonebooks! Bring out a stack of old phone books. Let the children use tape, scissors, and their imaginations to create something useful or artsy. Keep these creations at the library on display for a month or so. (For example, a secret pocket book to hide treasures inside or a chair.)

Closing to Parents:
We have a lot to learn about taking care of our planet. Please come see me if you want to learn more! See you again next week!

Additional Activity Ideas:

Online resources are available if you have internet access and a small group can use it!

Hard to recycle item search online recycle items such as glass, cell phones, and eye glasses.

Representatives of local organizations can be guest speakers if they can relate ways for this age group to get involved.

For schools, students can research environmental issues in groups and present to the class.

Recycled CD mobiles. For hanging in windows and reflecting sunlight.

This storytime was written by Stephanie G. Bauman.

Notes

Flight

Anticipated Length: 45 Minutes

Opening:

"Thanks for coming in today! How many of you been on an airplane? Today it might seem pretty normal to fly, but the invention of flight was complicated and amazing and full of adventure. So today we are going to learn a bit more about it."

Book Activity:
The Wright Brothers a Flying Start by Elizabeth MacLeod. ISBN# 1550749358
Real photos, easy to understand history of flight and the Wright brothers.

Activity:
Paper Airplane Creations
Use books or printouts from the internet to create sturdy paper airplanes. Each child colors paper and creates as many paper airplanes as they want.
Examples:

Kids' Paper Airplane Book by Ken Blackburn, Jeff Lammers, and Walter Chrynwski
Klutz Book of Paper Airplanes by Doug Stillinger
The Gliding Flight: 20 Excellent Fold and Fly Paper Airplanes by John M. Collins
Making Paper Airplanes That Really Fly by Nick Robinson

Book Activity:
Yankee Doodle Gals: Women Pilots of World War II by Amy Nathan.
ISBN# 0792282167
Read selections about female war heroes!

Paper Airplane Flying Contest
Have prizes ready. Winners can include: Best design, farthest flight, and trickiest flight.

Additional Activity Ideas:

Have a pilot come as guest speaker.
Learn more about flying today including careers in the industry.
Other modes of flight: blimp, hot air balloon, rocket man.
Watch a parachuting DVD.
Watch a Trick Pilot DVD.

This storytime was written by Stephanie G. Bauman.

From *Storytimes for Children* by Stephanie G. Bauman. Santa Barbara, CA: Libraries Unlimited. Copyright © 2011.

Geology

Anticipated Length: 45 Minutes

Opening:

"Hey everyone, glad to see you! Today we are going to talk about geology. You know, rocks! They are everywhere, so it's time to learn more about them!"

Book Activity:
1001 Facts about Rocks and Minerals by Sue Fuller and Chris Maynard.
ISBN# 0751344192 (Just read interesting and fun selections to bring up interest level)

Book Activity:
Let's Go Rock Collecting by Roma Gans. ISBN# 0064451704
Basic Rock formation, the use of rocks, and basic rock collecting.

Activity:
Guest Speaker with Samples
Arrange for a guest speaker from the local science museum or a school geology teacher. Ask them to bring *local* samples, so kids can rock hunt in their own backyards.

Book Activity:
Is There a Dinosaur in Your Backyard?: The World's Most Fascinating Fossils, Rocks, and Minerals by Spencer Christian. ISBN# 0471196169
More about rocks, but tied to the child's own backyard.

Activity:
Create a pet rock
Each child can pick a rock. It can be glued to a piece of felt. Sequins, jewels, and feathers can be glued to the rock. Glitter glue can add a name.

Closing to Parents:
Thanks for coming today! Next time you see a rock, pick it up and take a closer look! See you again next week!

Additional Activity Ideas:

Field trip outside with local rock books.
Maps to local rock hounding sites. Geodes, arrowheads, crystals.

This storytime was written by Stephanie G. Bauman.

Impressionist Art

Anticipated Length: 45 Minutes

Opening:

"Hey everyone, glad you came to the library today! Today we are going to talk about a type of artwork called Impressionism. You might have heard of some of the artists that did impressionist artwork: Renard, Degas, Monet, and Manet."

Book Activity:
Picture This! Activities and Adventures in Impressionism by Joyce Raimondo. ISBN# 0823025039

Activity:
Conduct a slide show or online slide show of famous impressionist art. What do the students like about the art? What don't they like?

Guest Speaker
Have a local artist come to speak. Someone who makes a living doing art in any of its many forms from creating paintings, pottery, or watercolors, to designing jewelry, furniture, interiors, or perhaps an architect who designs unusual buildings, to inspire the children about artist careers.

Book Activity:
Linnea in Monet's Garden by Cristina Bjork. ISBN# 9129583144
Great first-person art history account told by a child.

Activity:
The children can create their own impressionist artwork using paper and chalk or in the summer, on the sidewalk of the library.

Closing to Parents:
Thanks for coming today! Remember art and creating art comes in many forms, so be brave and create something that speaks to you! See you again next week!

Additional Activity Ideas:

Combine with a history lesson in the appropriate classroom.
Do some of the activities listed in the Picture This book.
Find out how the children can get involved in the local art scene
If there is a nearby art gallery, take a field trip.

This storytime was written by Stephanie G. Bauman.

 Notes

Inner Strength and Perseverance Booktalk

Anticipated Length: 45 Minutes

Opening:

"Today I am going to be telling you more about books we have here in the library. These stories all have one thing in common. They are about children your own age who posses inner strength and perseverance. When you are in a stressful situation it's your inner strength that can get you through. But what is that? Is it like a muscle that can be worked out? Let's get started."

Booktalks:
Read selected texts as well as giving concise and intriguing summaries.

1. **Among the Hidden** by Margaret Peterson Haddix. ISBN# 0689824750. Luke cannot go to school and must stay indoors. Why? Luke lives in a society where there is a law that only allows a family to have only two children and Luke is an illegal third child. His parents kept his existence a secret from everyone. Luke learns there are other third children in the world and joins their efforts in resisting the government that denies them the right to exist.
2. **A Series of Unfortunate Events: The Bad Beginning** by Lemony Snicket. ISBN# 006075589X. The three Baudelaire children, Sunny, Klaus, and Violet, suddenly find themselves orphans and homeless. As if that is not enough, they have been taken in by a man named Count Olaf, who poses as their uncle, but really turns out to be someone terrible. They must face one challenge after another to stay safe and stay alive. (Reading a short passage from any of this series will entice readers for all of the books.)
3. **Numbering All the Bones** by Ann Rinaldi. ISBN# 0786813784. This is a young girl's story of survival and bravery. Eulinda is thirteen years old and she is a slave on a Georgia plantation in 1864, as the Civil War is coming to an end. Her younger brother Zeke has been sold and her older brother Neddy leaves to fight for the North, leaving Eulinda alone to deal with the challenges of life as a slave and wondering if her brothers are okay.
4. **Bud, Not Buddy** by Christopher Paul Curtis. ISBN# 0553494104. Bud Caldwell is ten years old, motherless, and on the run, but he is not discouraged. He is on a journey to discover who his father is and he is sure his mother has left him clues to help him find the answer. He also has created his own set of rules to live by, rules for survival. Bud is not afraid of anything he may face and he will let nothing stand in the way of him uncovering the truth about his father.

5. **The Secret Garden** by Francis Hodgson Burnett. ISBN# 078582569X. Mary has lost both her parents to a plague in India and has now been shipped off to live with her uncle in the country. She is unhappy, rude and short with everyone, and has no friends. When she begins snooping around in her uncle's mansion, she discovers a young boy named Colin who believes he is dying. She convinces him he is not dying and begins taking him out on the grounds of the mansion for walks. Together they explore the many beautiful grounds and discover the "secret garden."

6. **Esperanza Rising** by Pam Munoz Ryan. ISBN# 0439398851. Esperanza's life was a good one in Mexico. She always had the fanciest dresses and servants to tend to her every need. Then tragedy strikes and Esperanza and her mother flee to California to become migrant workers. Esperanza is faced with hard labor, poverty, and prejudice for the first time. When her mother gets sick, she has to take on even more responsibility to make ends meet, and soon a strike for better working conditions threatens all that she holds dear in her new life.

Closing to Parents:
Looks like it's time to check out some books! Don't worry, we have more than one copy of each! See you next week!

This storytime is based closely on a storytime written by Melissa Castagna.

Magic Powers Booktalk

Anticipated Length: 45 Minutes

Opening:

"Today we are going to talk about magic powers! Harry Potter is not the only one with a bit of magic, so today I am going to tell you about some books that you might like about others with magic powers. First let's talk about magic powers."

Book Activity:
Eyewitness: Witches and Magic Makers by Douglas Hill. ISBN# 0789458780
Also see: http://en.wikipedia.org/wiki/List_of_superhuman_features_and_abilities_in_fiction

Booktalks:
(Read selected texts and provide concise and intriguing summaries.)

1. **Midnight for Charlie Bone** by Jenny Nimmo. ISBN# 0439474299. Charlie Bone discovers that he has a gift. He can hear people in photographs talking. The voices in the pictures introduce him to a mystery involving his father's past. Charlie's family soon sends him to Bloor's Academy where there are other "gifted" students. He makes friends and enemies at Bloor's, and learns the history of the Red Kind whose descendants still walk the earth. As Charlie attends the Academy and learns more about his own powers, he gets involved in a mysterious adventure that puts him right in the middle of the fight between good and evil.
2. **The Wish List** by Eoin Colfer. ISBN# 0439443369. Meg Finn's last act on earth was helping to rob an old man. She actually died in the attempt, but Meg is stuck in limbo, not bad enough for hell and not good enough for heaven. The only way for her to get into heaven is to go back to Earth and complete a task. She must help the old man she robbed. She must help him complete his "Wish List" with all the things he wants to do before he dies. If she can do that, then she can go to heaven. But there are other forces that will fight against her to thwart her efforts.
3. **Matilda** by Roald Dahl. ISBN# 0142410373. Matilda is smart, really smart, smarter than her own parents and she is just a little girl. She loves to read and learn and all her parents want her to do is watch TV. Her dad sells used cars for a living but he is a liar and a cheater and Matilda knows it. He has even lied about Matilda to Miss Trunchbull, the drill sergeant head mistress at Matilda's school, but Matilda won't let that get her down. She is determined to get rid of Miss Trunchbull and become the school hero. Can she do it?

Activity:
Palm Reading
Use palm reading books to have children take turns reading palms.

Closing to Parents:
Magic is such a great subject for authors to write about characters. Authors have created many characters and told their stories in books. Find them and get started reading!

Additional Activity Ideas:

Pick one "magic" power such as extra-sensory perception (ESP) and talk about the history and current status of this.

Scientific facts to support what magical powers are being proven true! An invisibility cloak is currently under study.

This storytime is based closely on a storytime written by Melissa Castagna.

 Notes

Musical Instruments

Anticipated Length: 1 Hour

Opening:

"Hello and welcome to the library! Today's theme is musical instruments and we are thrilled to have a guest musician to perform for us! I would like to start out by asking if any of you play a musical instrument. What do you play? How much time do you spend practicing? (Engage in a short discussion.)"

Our library has quite a few books that can help you find out about instruments and some that will introduce you to how to learn to play them. Here are a couple that you might find interesting.

Booktalks:

1. **Piano for Dummies** by Blake Neely. ISBN# 0470496444. This book starts at the beginning of learning how to play and helps the reader learn the basics of playing the piano. It comes with a CD to help you learn the sounds too.
2. **The First-Stage Guitar book** by Chris Lopez. ISBN# 0946771966. This is a great book for beginners. It shows you how to place your fingers on the strings and it helps you get started right away. It has some songs in it that you can learn how to play too.

Discussion:

Does anyone here know what an orchestra is? (Solicit answers.) An orchestra is a group of musicians playing their instruments together to make music. They all play the same song, but each sounds a little different. Together, they sound awesome!

Book Activity:

Those Amazing Musical Instruments! with CD: Your Guide to the Orchestra Through Sounds and Stories by Genevieve Helsby. ISBN# 1402208251

Song Activity:

The Violin's Ringing

http://www.songsforteaching.com/orchestrainstrumentsong.htm

I would like you to sing a song with me. It is really neat because we will divide up into sections just like an orchestra is divided, and we will sing the different parts of the orchestra. Let me show you. (Divide the group into instruments and have them sing their part.) Follow along on your song sheets.

Activity:
Guest Speaker
Invite anyone who plays an instrument professionally to come speak!

Discussion:
How can you get an instrument? They can be expensive! You can rent them, buy them used, or sometimes borrow them from your school. Even better is making your own instruments!

Activity:
Make Your Own Musical Instruments by Anna-marie D'cruz. ISBN# 1435829255
Students get to pick an instrument (pre-selection/materials pre-prepared).

Closing to Parents:
Thanks for coming today! You will find a display of music books in the children's room for you to have a look at. Thanks for coming to our musical storytime today!

Additional Activity Ideas:

Have a local music school or children's music group leader come to speak.
School: Download or purchase a music maker program for the computer, such as Garageband.

This storytime is based closely on a storytime written by Julie Andrews-Jotham.

Mysteries

Anticipated Length: 45 Minutes

Opening:

"Hello and welcome to our mystery club! We're glad you came to visit the library. Today, we will be reading some mysteries and having some fun. We'll even be going on a scavenger hunt! Our library has lots of mystery books that you might like to borrow. So, let's get started."

(Play some music on the CD player, such as the theme from Sherlock Holmes.)

Discussion:
What are some things that we like about mysteries? (Ask the children to come up with some words about mysteries and how they feel when they read them. Pass out pieces of card stock on which the children can write a descriptive word. These can be used for a bulletin board display for mysteries for the summer.)
Also talk about the elements of a mystery: http://www.readwritethink.org/lesson _images/lesson865/elements.pdf
http://www.seattlemystery.com/Definitions/definitions.html

Booktalks:
Mystery Books:

- Nancy Drew Series
- Hardy Boys Series
- An Enola Holmes Mystery (Series) by Nancy Springer

Introduce the main characters and talk about the theme and format of the books. Read an excerpt from one of each series.

Activity:
Movie
Young Sherlock Holmes (1985) Directed by Barry Levinson
Selected scenes: http://movieclips.com/or youtube.com.

Scavenger Hunt
Divide students into pairs and give each an envelope. Inside, they will be given a clue question, the answer to which will tell them where to begin the hunt. Each team will follow the clues until they complete all the questions on their sheet. Questions can be derived from the discussion and booktalks as well as the use of the library. Prizes will be awarded to all of those who complete their hunt. (Usually everyone does!) Go over the answers with the group and pass out the prizes.

Closing to Parents:
Thanks for coming to our storytime today! We hope that you had fun and that you will give some mysteries a try. See you next time.

Additional Activity Ideas:
The internet has many resources for this subject, here are some examples:

> Thinkquest—You're the Detective: http://library.thinkquest.org/5109/you_are _the_detective.html
> MysteryNet's Kids Mysteries: http://kids.mysterynet.com/solveit/

This storytime is based closely on a storytime written by Julie Andrews-Jotham.

Notes

Notes and Gossip

Anticipated Length: 45 Minutes

Opening:

"Hey everyone, glad to see you! Today we are going to talk about gossip and notes. Almost everyone gossips and passes notes!! Even me! But it can be really harmful, so it's important to talk about."

Book Activity:
Amelia's Book of Notes & Note Passing by Marissa Moss. ISBN# 0689874464
A fun story about the harm of gossip created by note passing.

Activity:
Note Passing Stories
The first child can each put one sentence on a piece of paper, then pass it on to the next person. When the paper is full, the story is done! (Instruct the last person to try to close up the story.) Read each of the stories the children have created together.

Discussion:
Why is gossip so interesting? It is a story about someone you usually know, and you find out something interesting but that may or may not be true. Sometimes part of the story is true, but another part is only a made up part or something that was misunderstood at the first hearing and is totally incorrect in the retelling. More often than not it becomes more like a story than something that really happened.

Activity:
The Whispered Story
The librarian starts with a 2–3 sentence long gossip snippet about a fictional child. Each child whispers what they can remember of it, and the final child says it aloud. This exercise illustrates how what really happened can change and become something very strange indeed.

Discussion:
The effects are much more harmful than a story made up for fun and entertainment. Is there a time when gossip is acceptable? What about if it's about a movie star, or someone you will never see again, like a stranger at an airport? Is gossiping a form of bullying?

Book Activity:
Gossip: Deal With It Before Word Gets Around by Catherine Rondina.
ISBN# 1435278895

Closing to Parents:
I hope that gave everyone something to think about! See you again next week!

Additional Activity Ideas:
Many great books are available on this subject! Here is a start:

> **Speak Up and Get Along!: Learn the Mighty Might, Thought Chop, and More Tools to Make Friends, Stop Teasing, and Feel Good About Yourself** by Scott Cooper. ISBN# 1575421828

This storytime was written by Stephanie G. Bauman.

 Notes

Scary Reader's Theatre and Spooky Stories

Anticipated Length: 1 Hour

Opening:

"Welcome everyone. Today we are planning to get a little scary! We are going to tell ghost stories and even better, participate in a reader's theatre to act out a scary tale! It doesn't have to be Halloween to be a good time to get scared!"

Activity:
Local Hauntings!
I use a map and a flashlight, and anything off the internet to present local haunted places and stories.

Discussion:
Why do people want to believe in ghosts? Are they real? (Keep this discussion light and non-secular. It's fun to be scared, but you don't want the children to have nightmares!)

Book Activity:
Mysteries Unwrapped: Haunted U.S.A. by Charles Wetzel. ISBN# 1402737351

Discussion:
Today we are going to put on a play! Let's review the roles and get all set up!

Activity:
Scary Readers Theatre by Suzanne Barchers. ISBN# 1563082926
This book contains 30 folk tales, myths, and legends for reader's theatre and it includes readability and scariness ratings. Numbered script lines assist readers in their line delivery. Scripts are reproducible so produce one for each member of the group. Props could be chosen from the library dress-up trunk although you really don't need any props at all. Your listeners can make props with their imaginations.

Closing to Parents:
Thanks for coming everyone! We have many books of ghost stories and supernatural tales here at the library if you are interested! (We generally finish this program with snacks and a review of what we did.) Perhaps we could look through the book and choose a story for the next visit?

This storytime is based closely on a storytime written by Julie Andrews-Jotham.

 Notes

School House Booktalk

Anticipated Length: 45 Minutes

Opening:

"Good morning! Today I am going to share with you three chapter books. They all are set in a school. What do you think would happen in your class if all of a sudden your teacher disappeared? Would things go on as normal or would there be a giant party? Teacher, what do you think would happen?"

Booktalks:

1. **The Secret School** by Avi. ISBN: 0152046992. That is exactly what happens in our first book. The title of this book is *The Secret School*. It is written by Avi. The story is historical fiction. That means is it set in historical times, not in your lifetime. The story takes place in a small country school where all the students in all grades share one class room and one teacher. One day the teacher announces to the students that her mother is gravely ill and she must go back home to take care of her. It is close to the end of the school year and the school board decides it will be impossible to find another teacher so late in the year so they decide to close the school and have all the students repeat the grade the following year! That's like every student in the entire school gets held back!

   For one of the students, Ida, this would wreck her plans to become a teacher herself. So what if Ida, who is the oldest and smartest student in the school, became the teacher? Could she teach the others and herself as well? Could they keep it a secret so the school board wouldn't close the school? All they have to do is study hard (They have the books.) and pass the test at the end of the year. Do you think they can do it? You will have to read the book to find out.

2. **Flying Solo** by Ralph Fletcher. ISBN: 0395873231. Do you know what happens if a teacher calls in sick? We have a system and the teacher calls the system and the system then calls a substitute to come in. But what happens if the substitute who is supposed to show up, doesn't show up? What happens then? The title of the book is *Flying Solo*, by Ralph Fletcher, and that is exactly what happens in this story. The sixth graders show up for class one day and there is no teacher and no substitute either. They wait, and wait, and finally they realize no teacher is coming. Should they tell someone? Of course, they should, but wait, what if no one finds out, what then? How do they keep anyone from finding out? Throwing a party probably isn't the best way to keep it a secret. So they decide to act like the teacher *is* there. Do you think it would work? How long do you think they can pull it off? Oh yeah, one more thing: there is a student in the class who doesn't talk. She can

talk, but she has decided not to talk. Do you think that might add to the difficulties? You will have to read the book to find out.

3. **No Talking** by Andrew Clements. ISBN: 9780545054362. The third book I want to share with you is about a class with a bad reputation. They are not bad kids. They just love to talk and talk and talk. Sound familiar? And not only that, they are very competitive, especially the boys against the girls. One day, one of the boys decides to see how long he can go without talking, just for fun. After a while, others find out what he is doing and the competition begins. First, one girl finds out and she is sure no boy could possibly go longer without talking than any girl. So they all agree to see who can go the longest without talking, the boys or the girls. Of course, they have to decide on the rules, what if a teacher calls on you? Does that count if you have to answer? Who is going to keep track? How long will this go on? It doesn't take long before the teachers start to notice something is different. Isn't this the class that talks nonstop? What's wrong with them? The teachers get nervous because they can't figure out what is going on. The principal decides to demand that they start talking, if you can believe it! So who do you think wins the boys or the girls? You will have to read the book to find out.

Closing to Parents:
I hope I have shown you some books that some of you might like to read. Two of the authors, Andrew Clements and Avi have both written several books and they write great books, so check out their other titles.

This storytime is based on a storytime written by Elizabeth Turner.

Stargazing

Anticipated Length: 45 Minutes

Opening:

"Hi everyone and welcome to our program about stars and the night sky. Our library has lots of books about astronomy, the study of the stars, and stories too. Let's look at a few of them and read a little and then I will introduce our special guest."

Opening Song:

Harvest Moon, by Neil Young (playing as we assemble)

Booktalks:

Read selections from each as well.

1. **Out-of-this-World Astronomy** by Joe Rhatigan, Rain Newcomb, and Greg Doppmann. ISBN# 1579906753. This is an excellent book, written by a middle school teacher. It contains over 300 awesome photos and 50 fantastic projects. It has a great deal of information and it tries to answer questions that you might have about astronomy. Maybe you could do a project for the science fair about astronomy?
2. **Eyewitness Astronomy** by Kristen Lippincott. ISBN# 0789448882. This is a typical eyewitness book, full of wonderful pictures and information about astronomy. It even has a CD and a wall chart that help you identify items in the night sky. Our library has the entire series of eyewitness books. They are always filled with interesting facts and beautiful photos and illustrations.

Book Activity:

The North Star by Peter Reynolds. ISBN# 0763636770. Now I would like to read a bit from a book called The North Star. This book isn't literally about stars, but it encourages readers to observe, wonder, and consider choosing your own path, to pursue your dreams. I think you'll like it. (Read a few selections).

Activity:

Guest Speaker

Invite a local astronomer, astronomy professor/teacher, or even an enthusiast to come speak. Hopefully they can bring a small telescope as well.

Additional Activity Ideas:

Provide coloring sheets for phases of the moon or for the planets in our solar system
Recreate our solar system at scale having children use a variety of balls.
Learn more about shooting stars.
Learn how to travel by starlight. How to find the North Star.
Use a night sky creator to project stars onto the ceiling.

This storytime is based on a storytime written by Julie Andrews-Jotham.

 Notes

The Bayou

Anticipated Length: 45 Minutes

Opening:
(Play some Cajun music)

"Hi Everyone! Thanks for coming today. We are going to be talking about the bayou. That is a special kind of swampland in the state of Louisiana. An entire culture and language has developed in that area that is unique and special. We are going to learn a bit about that and then put on a play about animals that live in the Bayou."

Have you ever been on the ride at Disneyland called Pirates of the Caribbean? The first part of that ride is through the bayou. They also visit the bayou in the movies of the same name. Let's get started.

Book Activity:
Cajuns and Their Acadian Ancestors: A Young Reader's History by Shane K. Bernard. ISBN# 1934110787
(Read selected passages.)

Activity:
Make a Cookbook
Provide a selection of Cajun/Creole recipes from the internet that are simple and easy. Talk about each one and show a picture. As allowed, bring homemade cornbread. Students can pick and choose which recipes to include. They can create a cover then bind it together with string or yarn through pre-punched holes.

Book Activity:
Haunted Bayou by J. J. Reneaux. ISBN# 087483385X
(Read selected stories. Dim the lights and play cricket music).

Activity:
Readers Theater
Gator Gumbo: A Spicy Hot Tale by Candace Fleming. ISBN# 0374380503
Characters: Narrator, Gator, Possum, Skunk, Otter. (You could use pairs of readers for the possums, skunks, and otters in order to incorporate more children.)
Props: A cane for gator because he is old, a flower for skunk because she smells so "sweet," a baseball cap for possum, and a slingshot for otter.
Have scripts for the characters with their parts highlighted.
Have students act out story as they read.

Closing to Parents:
I hope you had a good time today. I look forward to seeing you next week. Enjoy your books boys and girls.

Additional Activity Ideas:

Learn about Mardi Gras.
Learn about Hurricane Katrina.
Learn about cajun and jazz music.
Is there any local swampland? Learn more about it.
Have a local petshop/animal handler bring in a baby alligator.

This storytime is based closely on a storytime written by Elizabeth Turner.

Notes

Trees

Anticipated Length: 45 Minutes

Opening:

"Hello Everyone! Today we are talking about trees and how important they are to this world! You may have heard about the destruction of the rainforest, and how that is affecting climate change. We are going to learn about why that is, and what you can do about protecting and caring for trees."

Book Activity:
The Giving Tree by Shel Silverstein. ISBN# 0060586753
Learn about what we take from trees and how valuable they truly are.

Book Activity:
Tree (DK Eyewitness Books) by David Burnie. ISBN# 075661094X
(Read selections.)

Activity:
Tree Anatomy
http://www.enchantedlearning.com/subjects/plants/printouts.shtml
(Have children label the part of trees.)

Book Activity:
The Life Cycle of a Tree by Bobbie Kalman and Kathryn Smithyman.
ISBN# 0778706893

Book Activity:
Why Save the Rain Forest? by Donald M. Silver. ISBN# 0671866109

Activity:
Identify Local Trees
Your local government agency can provide you with a guide to local trees, or there are many resources available online. Have the children identify trees out the window or take a trip outside to learn more.

Closing to Parents:
Thanks for coming today! I hope everyone can take an active part in caring for trees and helping to protect our planet. I hope to see you all next week!

Additional Activity Ideas:

Vist the Web site for Arbor Day http://www.arborday.org/explore/ (This Web site is full of activities and ways to get involved.)

Visit the Web site for National Geographic, which has lots of useful information and stunning imagery.

http://ngm.nationalgeographic.com/redwoods/redwoods

http://environment.nationalgeographic.com/environment/habitats/rainforest-profile.html

Have a local arborist come in to talk about how to care for trees and local trees.

Plant a small tree on the grounds of the library or school.

This storytime is based loosely on a storytime written by Kathy Burgener.

Notes

Unwanted Responsibilities Booktalk

Anticipated Length: 45 Minutes

Opening:

"Today I am going to be telling you more about books we have here in the library. These books all have one thing in common, they are unwanted responsibilities. Like taking out the trash! Ugh! Sometimes you have to prove yourself to get a responsibility that you want, such as getting a puppy. Other times it comes up whether you are ready or not, such as middle school or junior high. Let's get started."

Booktalks:

Read selected texts and give concise and intriguing summaries.

1. **Ender's Game** by Orson Scott Card. ISBN# 0812550706. Would you want the weight of the world on your shoulders? As the second war with the enemy alien race, the "Buggers," approaches, the search is on for a new leader. The government thinks they have found their leader in 6-year-old Andrew "Ender" Wiggin. Ender enters battle school up in space where armies are formed to fight mock battles to teach the students combat skills. He rises quickly through the ranks despite being the target of bullying and it is not long before Ender is commanding his own pretend army; but is he ready to command the armies of the Earth against the Buggers? The adults think so, but Ender isn't so sure.

2. **Percy Jackson and the Olympians: The Lightning Thief** by Rick Riordan. ISBN# 0786838655. What happens if you can't handle it when you are given a giant helping of responsibility? Percy Jackson keeps getting in to trouble and getting kicked out of school. The crazy things that are happening to him aren't his fault and he doesn't know why monsters keep attacking him. Then he finds out that he is a demigod, the son of Poseidon, and that Zeus's lightning bolt has been stolen and Percy is the prime suspect. He has just a few days to figure out the truth and return Zeus's lightning bolt or literally total chaos will break loose. This book is packed with excitement and adventure; you will be on the edge of your seat wondering how Percy will get out of this mess.

3. **Scepter of the Ancients (Skulduggery Pleasant)** by Derek Landy. ISBN# 0061231177. What happens when a normal responsibility turns out to be much more than you bargained for? Stephanie is shocked to learn that she inherited all of her uncle's grand estate. But she soon learns that her Uncle was mixed up in a supernatural world that includes one of her uncle's friends named Skulduggery Pleasant, a walking, talking, fire-throwing skeleton with great fashion sense. Not only has she inherited her uncle's estate, she's also inherited some of his problems. Stephanie, with Skulduggery at her side, soon finds herself in the middle of the battle between

good and evil and must help save the world from Skulduggery's old nemesis, the evil Serpine.

4. **Ranger's Apprentice: The Ruins of Gorlan** by John Flanagan. ISBN# 0142406635. In this book the main character is prepared to take on responsibility but it doesn't turn out the way he hoped. In Will's world, everybody becomes the apprentice to somebody at the age of 15. Will never knew what he was supposed to be, so like most of the other boys, he aspires to be a warrior. But this was not to be. Instead, he is chosen to be an apprentice to a Ranger. The Rangers are a cloak-wearing, shadowy, mysterious lot who make Will nervous. Will soon comes to realize that the Rangers, with their keen observations, their survival skills, and their talent to move about unseen, are instrumental in the war against the evil Lord Morgarath.

Closing to Parents:
Looks like it's time to check out some books! Don't worry, we have more than one copy of each!
See you next week!

Additional Activity Ideas:

Are you ready to move up in school? Have an older child from middle or junior high come speak.

What could you do if you wanted to earn a little extra money?

What responsibilities do you want that you don't have? What can you do to get them?

This storytime is based on a storytime written by Melissa Castagna.

Who Let the Dogs Out? Booktalk

Anticipated Length: 45 Minutes

Opening:

"**G**ood morning boys and girls. Who likes dogs? Who likes cats? I like both, but today, I am going to share some books about dogs. Has anyone read, *Where the Red Fern Grows* or seen the movie? (I use this example because this is a book our fifth graders read.) What happens to the dogs in that story? (Sadly, they die.) How do you feel when animals die in books?"

Opening Music:
Chorus from: *Who Let the Dogs Out?* by Baha Men. (Other Lyrics inappropriate) or *How Much is That Doggie in the Window?* originally sung by Patti Page but there are several versions out there you can download. I think the kids would relate better to *Who Let the Dogs Out?*

Booktalks:

1. **Because of Winn-Dixie** by Kate DiCamillo. ISBN# 0763607762. The first book I am going to share with you is about a dog and first of all, I will tell you right up front the dog does not die in this book. The title of the book is, *Because of Winn-Dixie*. The main character in the story is a girl. She lives with her father in Florida and doesn't have too many friends. She encounters a dog in the grocery store and in order to save the dog from being taken to the pound she claims the dog belongs to her. She names the dog Winn-Dixie because that is the name of store where she meets the dog. Together these two friends have lots of adventures and make other new friends. If you like dogs, this is a fun book with a good story, and you may still be able to rent the movie to see at home.
2. **My Life in Dog Years** by Gary Paulsen, Gary. ISBN# 0385325703. This is a book of short stories about dogs. I will warn you though some of these dogs do die, but some of the stories are funny, some are sad, some are scary. The title is, *My Life in Dog Years*. The author tells stories about all the dogs he has had in his lifetime. (Read pages 67–81 about a Great Dane named Caesar.)
3. **Love That Dog** by Sharon Creech. ISBN: 0060292873. In our next book, the boy in the story doesn't like poetry and he has a teacher that loves it and wants the students to write poetry. I think I would have a hard time in that class. Would you? The teacher has the students keep a journal and write in it regularly. The teacher asks Jack, the boy in the story, if he has a pet? Jack says he used to have a pet, but he doesn't want to write about it. The she suggests he write about a pet he would like to have. Jack doesn't like this idea either. You go through most of the book

trying to figure out what happened to Jack's pet and wondering if he is going to learn to appreciate poetry or will Jack and teacher be forever at odds with each other.

4. **Gully's Travels** by Tom Seidler. ISBN: 9780545125065. Another fun book about a dog is a new book called, *Gully's Travels*, by Tor Seidler. The dog in this story has it made. Life is perfect for the dog until his master falls in love and is going to get married. The problem is the lady is allergic to the dog, so the master decides to give the dog away. The new home is different from his previous life. He is not happy, he misses his old life so he tries to sneak back home. Eventually though, he accepts his new home and things settle down a little; but things aren't going well back at his old house either, so Gulliver gets to go back home! Will he be happy or will he miss all the hustle and bustle of life with a family? Where will he end up?

Closing to Parents:
These are just a few books we have about dogs. Some are funny, some are sad, some are long, some are short, some are true, and some are fiction. So if you like dogs there is a book out there for you. I hope you enjoy your books and I will see you next week.

Additional Activity Ideas:

Movie: **My Dog Skip** (Warner Home Video 2000).

This storytime is based on a storytime written by Elizabeth Turner.

6

Pre-Teens (11–12 Year Olds)

Traditional storytimes will not work for this notoriously picky age group, if you read them a long story they are likely to zone out or entertain themselves by texting (if they are not forbidden in their classroom if this is for a school). Keep them involved and their brains active by presenting fun and engaging learning activities that are relevant to their lives. Demonstrations and interactive participation with current services offered by the library are also perfect, such as showing off the newest age-geared photo imaging program. If your storytimes program is in conjunction with curriculum, add an extra element through webquests online, and video snippets. To find success with the Pre-Teens give them a little, be there to guide, and let them roll with it!

Archeology

Anticipated Length: 45 Minutes

Opening:

"**W**elcome to the library. Today we are going to talk about archeology. This is the study of ancient people and their cultures. In the United States anthropologists study many cultures from Native Americans to pilgrims. You can love archeology without wanting to be an archeologist when you grow up. Learning about history, especially new discoveries about history can be really fun and interesting."

Book Activity:
Archeology (DK Eyewitness Books) by Jane McIntosh. ISBN# 0789458640
(Read selections.)

Book Activity:
Archaeology for Kids: Uncovering the Mysteries of Our Past, 25 Activities
by Richard Panchyk. ISBN# 1556523955
(Read selections, or conduct a variety of activities suggested in the book.)

Activity:
Trash Can Dig
http://www.nps.gov/history/archeology/PUBLIC/kids/index.htm
Most of archeology consists of looking at trash! What can trash tell us about a person or group of people?

Book Activity:
North American Indian (DK Eyewitness Books) by David S. Murdoch. ISBN# 0756610818

Activity:
Web Exploration on Native Americans
http://www.native-languages.org/kids.htm
Children explore the various resources on the site. If there are tribes in the area, the activity can be narrowed down to the specific group.

Closing to Parents:
Thanks for coming today! I hope you learned a lot about archeology and Native Americans and found some great books to read!

Additional Activity Ideas:
See these great web resources:

http://www.dmoz.org/Kids_and_Teens/School_Time/Social_Studies/Archaeology/

http://www.pbs.org/wgbh/nova/teachers/resources/subj_01_00.html

Guest Speaker: Invite a local anthropologist, archeologist, or even paleontologist to speak.

This storytime was written by Stephanie G. Bauman.

 Notes

Body Image!

Anticipated Length: 1 Hour

Opening:

"Today we are going to talk about body image. Do you ever stop to think about where standards of what people should look like come from? Should you sacrifice your health to be a bodybuilder? How do you know if you are at your personal best? Sometimes we are told to "accept ourselves" but we know that sometimes we don't like ourselves! Examining and talking about where perceptions come from, can go a long way to helping us understand how we see and feel about ourselves. Let's think about how and why we feel and how others you know may feel about their image."

Book Activity:

No Body's Perfect: Stories by Teens about Body Image, Self-Acceptance, and the Search for Identity by Kimberly Kirberger. ISBN# 0439426383
(Read selections.)

Discussion/Activity:

1. Look at the Web site: http://kidshealth.org/teen/your_body/ and discuss.
2. Can your body affect your life? What about being overweight? What about having acne? What if someone feels ugly? What about people who feel they are overweight, but really aren't? (List other "problems" on a whiteboard.) Do you know anyone who stutters? Is making remarks about the way someone looks a form of bullying?
3. Influences on our image or our body
   Parents
   Peers
   Media (historically, present, television ads)
   History of Body Image: http://www.peelregion.ca/health/commhlth/bodyimg/
      media.htm
   Today—What does everyone want to look like? Is it possible?
   Types—toys (Barbie, GI Joe), TV, movies, ads.
   Stats on media and body image http://www.nationaleatingdisorders.org/p.asp?
      WebPage_ID=286&Profile_ID=41166
4. What can be done about some of these problems? Can someone change their body and how they look?
   Plastic Surgery. http://abcnews.go.com/Entertainment/popup?id=8635003
   Discuss: Genetics, metabolism, Thyroid Conditions
   What happens if you go too far?

Steroids http://www.teendrugabuse.us/teensteroids.html

Anorexia or bulimia http://kidshealth.org/teen/food_fitness/problems/eat
_disorder.html

Activity:
Media Influence

Find ads that depict people from a variety of sources. Online, magazines, and book covers. Present to the group for discussion on what is realistic and what is not. What would have been better?

Discussion:
Acceptance (for yourself and others). Takes confidence and mostly bravery!
What is the worst thing that can happen if you accept someone as they are? If you accept yourself? How to put *acceptance into action*?

Additional Activity Ideas:

   Using media clippings from donated magazines create a healthy CollageVision of themselves!
   Guest Speaker: In order to facilitate discussion on the repercussion of poor body image/self-worth invite someone from a suicide hotline or an anorexia center.
   In groups, find an magazine ad that might affect body image and re-create it to better meet the body image needs of the public as well as sell the product better.

This storytime was written by Stephanie G. Bauman.

Change Your World

Anticipated Length: 1 Hour

Opening:

"**I**n our time together today, we are going to talk about how you can change the world!"

Activity:
World Issues

1. Discussion: What issues in the world today strike a cord with you? What worries you? Upsets you? Why should you care about what is happening?
2. Web search: Each student does a web search on an issue that worries them. What is the latest news that you find difficult to understand and difficult for anyone to solve?
3. Discussion: Divide into groups based on topic (e.g., human/animal/environment). In these groups the children will share their resources and talk about what they found. As a full group, discuss how these issues are interrelated (e.g., poverty relates to hunger relates to infant death rates).

Book Activity:
The Teen Guide to Global Action: How to Connect with Others (Near & Far) to Create Social Change by Barbara A. Lewis. ISBN# 1575422662

Activity:
State Issues

1. Students individually and in small groups will research online for local non-profits/agencies that deal with their issues. Then the entire group will make a longer list. The group will choose their top three and all contact information will be noted. Does their Web sites tell how youth can get involved?
2. How to get involved. What's the next step? Call? Write? Email? Try to raise money? (Non-profits can be contacted to find out what resources, opportunities, and ideas they have for pre-teens. Maybe arrange for a guest speaker if there is enough interest on that issue.)

Activity:
Down to the Individual
Children will explore the Web site: www.earthskids.com/change. They will each choose one student they find a connection to and create a short email or letter to that student

that could include: What they have in common, what they think is neat about what the student accomplished, how they are going to help with a similar issue in their own community.

Book Activity:
What's It Like Living Green?: Kids Teaching Kids, by the Way They Live by Jill Ammon Vanderwood. ISBN# 1439224773
(Read selections.)

Discussion:
The group will talk about any additional ideas or questions that they have about making a difference right now, such as ask for holiday gifts to go to a charity, knowing how to deal with local wildlife, picking up garbage while hiking, or volunteering with parent.

Additional Activity Ideas:

Children can create a blog of how they helped a local charity/ongoing. Does the library have a project/partnership with a local charity that children can be a part of?

This storytime was written by Stephanie G. Bauman.

Crime Scene Detectives

Anticipated Length: 1 Hour

Opening:

 "**T**oday we are going to talk about crime and punishment. This may sound like the title of a stuffy classical novel, but we are going to talk about real crime, crime scenes, and even bodies!"

Book Activity:
Forensic Science (DK Eyewitness Books) by Christopher Cooper. ISBN# 0756633834
All the interesting ways to solve a crime using evidence.
(Read selections.)

Crime and Detection (DK Eyewitness Books) by Brian Lane. ISBN# 0756613868
A history of crime fighting techniques are discussed.

Book Activity:
Stiff: The Curious Lives of Human Cadavers by Mary Roach. ISBN# 0393324826.
This humorous book describes the wide variety of ways that a dead human body can be useful.
(Read selections.)

Activity:
Murder Mystery Party
Murder Mystery Party Games: Panic at the Prom for Teens by Universal Games or Murder Mystery Party—Lethal Luau by Universal Games
Also see: http://www.dinnerandamurder.com/games/kids.htm
These are a super amount of fun! You can also create your own, and tie in fact finding to the library resources.

Closing to Parents:
Thanks for coming in today. If you like to think about solving crimes or even a mystery, you can research this as a career. If you want to know more, come and see me and we will help you find those resources. Have a great day!

Additional Activity Ideas:

Free Online Games: Try searching for "crime scene online games" and see what comes up. New ones pop up everyday and old ones disappear. They are usually pretty simple but sometimes have older age content, so play it through first.

Example:

http://www.virtualmuseum.ca/Exhibitions/Myst/en/game/index.phtml
http://www.platospond.com/
http://www.yourdiscovery.com/crime/csi/

Booktalk on **Half Moon Investigations** by Eoin Colfer. ISBN 0786849576. Eoin takes an online detective course, but will it be useful when he is hired by a popular girl at school to solve a mystery? The writing is silly and fun!
Guest Speaker: Invite someone from criminal justice, even someone who does fingerprinting would be interesting.

This storytime was written by Stephanie G. Bauman.

 Notes

Journaling

Anticipated Length: 1 Hour

Opening:

"Our topic today will be journals and it's not all 'dear diary,' there is a lot more to recording your life, thoughts, and ideas than a tiny book with a key."

Activity:
The Stereotypical Journal

1. Read aloud selections from Anne Frank's journal and visit History: The Anne Frank Center USA
2. Read aloud selections from any other journals in both book form and from the internet. (I have both family journals of distant relatives, pioneers, my mother's journal as a young hipster in New York city, and my own personal journals).

Discussion:
Characteristics of a Journal

Who can write a journal? How is a journal different from an autobiography? Discuss fictional journals, such as those portrayed in Bridget Jones' Diary or Princess Diaries.

Do men keep journals? History of Journals: http://en.wikipedia.org/wiki/Diary #History

What should be in a journal? Why should you keep a journal? The danger of a journal.

Activity:
The Modern Journal—The Blog

1. Discussion
    What is a blog? What can it be used for? Compare and contrast to journal.
2. How to Create your own Blog for Free!
    Safety Tips: http://www.microsoft.com/protect/parents/social/blogging.aspx
    No One Cares What You Had for Lunch: 100 Ideas for Your Blog by Margaret Mason. ISBN#032144972X
    (Read selections.)
3. Blog Search:
    Each Preteen conducts a search for blogs that are interesting to them: a famous persons, a favorite show, an author, a hobby, a condition (e.g., if they are diabetic).

4. Discussion:

> What did they like? What didn't you like? What caught your attention? What shows good safety? What's doesn't? What would you do to improve it? Any really interesting features?

Activity:

Your Own Blog (Or a Class Blog/Library Blog)

This can be started in the library or just a how-to discussion with an idea book started by each Preteen. They can decide as a group on the features they want to include. Examples: book reviews, student profiles, with anonymous pictures, events (school, library, or home) or place profiles, hobby talk, food reviews, pet pictures, and descriptions.

Additional Activity Ideas:

> Those Preteens who start a blog should let the librarian know so they can be linked to library sites for other Preteens, especially if they are reviewing books, movies, and using technology.

> For a school project, Preteens can create a how-to list about blogging for students their age, with suggestions, pictures, links and advice. This can be printed or go up on the school Web site.

> For a school project, students can research and create a blog style school paper. They can interview and accept contributors from other classrooms. The students decide on who plays what role and what types of articles they should publish.

This storytime was written by Stephanie G. Bauman.

Nutrition

Anticipated Length: 45 Minutes

Opening:

"**T**oday we are going to talk about why you should care what you eat!"

Activity:
What Do You Eat?
Children fill out a chart of the past three days of food. Then they log how many calories the meal had.
Nutritional Information of Produce: http://www.produceoasis.com/Alpha_Folder/Alpha.html
Nutritional content of food: http://www.webmd.com/diet/healthtool-food-calorie-counter

Activity:
What Should You Eat?

1. Examine the food pyramids
      Regular Food Pyramid: http://www.nutritionexplorations.org/kids/nutrition-pyramid.asp
      Vegetarian Food Pyramid: http://www.sos.org/webpage/veg/Nutrition.html
2. Create a personalized Food Pyramid:
      http://www.mypyramid.gov/mypyramid/index.aspx
3. Discussion:
      Are you meeting your current nutritional needs?

Book Activity:
The Omnivore's Dilemma for Kids: The Secrets behind What You Eat by Michael Pollan. ISBN# 0803735006
(Read selections.)

Activity:
Why Should I Care?
(The teacher librarian will present a short refresher on legitimate Web sites, authentic Web sites, and accurate Web sites.)

1. Preteens research online databases, or newspaper articles, Web sites on poor nutrition in groups of two. Each group then presents their results to the entire group answering the question, "Why is this source accurate?"

Activity:
What Can I Do About It?

1. How should you plan for your lifestyle: What you want to do? Who you want to be? (You can discuss major fields such as business, law, medicine, service professions, sports, and music.) How will what you choose to do affect your nutrition needs? (Depending upon the role in business, many will sit at a desk and not require the same amount of food to sustain themselves, etc.)
2. Preteens will log in and create a personal menu.
   Personal Menu Planner: http://www.mypyramidtracker.gov/planner/launchPage.aspx

Closing to Parents:
Thanks for coming today! Let's not eat better because some agency tells us to. Let's do it for ourselves. So we can be alert, smart, full of energy, and able to live the lifestyle we want to. The library has many books on nutrition, as well as many cookbooks, so check them out!

Additional Activity Ideas:

In groups of two, Preteens will find 10 healthy snacks via online searches. This will create one giant document to print for each participant.

Create restaurant menus based on lifestyle, such as for athletes, for students, for insomniacs. To do this, have them create fictitious people on the personal menu planner: http://www.mypyramid.gov/mypyramid/index.aspx

What about vitamins/supplements? Do they work? When are they needed? Side effects?

Read: *Eat Fresh Food: Awesome Recipes for Teen Chefs* by Rozanne Gold. ISBN# 1599904454

This storytime was written by Stephanie G. Bauman.

Sleep and Dreams

Anticipated Length: 45 Minutes

Opening:

"Today we are going to talk about sleeping and dreaming. This is something that everyone has in common! Every living creature on this planet sleeps and many of them dream, we think! Even sharks sleep, but they always keep moving. The worst is falling asleep when you are not supposed to or not being able to fall asleep when you need to or want to. Dreaming is interesting too, a lot of people have ideas about why we dream, but no one knows for sure. Sometimes it can be fun, and sometimes really scary. Let's find out more!"

Book Activity:
Zzz . . . : The Most Interesting Book You'll Ever Read about Sleep (Mysterious You). by Trudee Romanek. ISBN# 1550749463

Discussion:
When someone falls asleep in school is it their fault or the teacher's? What solutions can you think of? (examples: allowing students to stand up, go get a drink, take a hall walk, do a refreshing set of jumping jacks).

Activity:
Sleep Information Web sites
http://kidshealth.org/teen/food_fitness/wellbeing/how_much_sleep.html
http://www.sleepfoundation.org/article/sleep-topics/teens-and-sleep

Discussion:
How many people dream? Can you remember them? Are they in color? Do you know you are dreaming? This is called lucid dreaming. We are going to learn more about dreams. Here are some theories about why people dream:
http://www.psychologytoday.com/blog/the-literary-mind/200911/why-do-we-dream

Book Activity:
The Mystery Library: Dreams by Stuart A. Kallen. ISBN# 159018288X
(Read selections.)

Activity:
Dream Interpretation
Using a variety of sources from the web, to texts, to guessing students pair off to do dream interpretation.

The Complete Book of Dreams (DK Living) by Julia Parker and Derek Parker. ISBN# 0789432951

The Dream Book: A Young Person's Guide to Understanding Dreams by Patricia Garfield. ISBN# 0887765947

Dream interpreter: http://www.thecuriousdreamer.com/

Closing to Parents:

Thanks for coming today. I hope you learned a lot about sleep and dreaming. Remember that what really matters is that you are getting enough sleep for you! If you are a night owl, plan now for a career that will allow you to do that!

Additional Activity Ideas:

> How to keep a dream journal
> What to do if you have sleep problems
> Does caffeine really help? What are the risks!

This storytime was written by Stephanie G. Bauman.

The Evolution of Writing

Anticipated Length: 1 Hour

Opening:

"**D**o you know how writing has evolved over thousands of years? That's what we are going to learn about today."

Activity:
Cave Pictures
Cave of Lascaux: The Cave of Prehistoric Wall Paintings by Brad Burnham. ISBN# 0823962571
(Read selections.)
Chauvet Cave in France: http://ngm.nationalgeographic.com/ngm/data/2001/08/01/html/ft_20010801.6.html

Discussion:
Did ancient people create cave paintings just for art or were they communicating?

Activity:
Hieroglyphics—Egyptian and Mayan
Writing in Ancient Egypt (Writing in the Ancient World) by Jill Fine. ISBN# 0823965066
(Read selections.)
Egyptian Hieroglyphics: http://is.gd/6Ha87
Mayan Hieroglyphics: http://www.mayankids.com/mmkpeople/mkwrite.htm

Discussion:
Would this have been easy to read? Some languages, like Japanese, still show some forms of pictographs. They are symbols for whole words!

Activity:
Illuminated Books—Middle Ages
Magic in the Margins: A Medieval Tale of Bookmaking by W. Nikola-Lisa. ISBN# 0618496424
(Read selections.)
Overview of Writing: http://medievalwriting.50megs.com/literacy/writing.htm
Illuminated Manuscripts: http://www.historicpages.com/texts/mshist.htm

Activity:
Write on Parchment
Copy a favorite poem or quote onto a piece of parchment (or heavy paper). Use a calligraphy pen and inks.

Closing to Parents:
Next came typed and bound books by machine's called printing presses so everyone could have a copy! What is writing like today? Much is done on computers. There are even e-books? Will libraries disappear?
I was glad to see everyone today! We have more history books and even a few on calligraphy for you to take away if you would like.

Additional Activity Ideas:

Other resources on Egyptian hieroglyphics:http://egypt.mrdonn.org/hieroglyphics .html
Writing tools through the ages: http://www.ringpen.com/history.html
Book: **Scribes, Script, and Books: The Book Arts from Antiquity to the Renaissance** by Leila Avrin. IBSN# 0838910386

This storytime was written by Stephanie G. Bauman.

Vampires

Anticipated Length: 1 Hour

Opening:

"Today during the time you are in the library we are going to talk about vampires. They are a really popular topic right now and you can find great interest in movies and books about them. Really what's not to like? They live forever young, are usually really handsome or beautiful, and are strong. So let's learn more about vampires."

Book Activity:

Encyclopedia Horrifica: The Terrifying TRUTH! About Vampires, Ghosts, Monsters, and More By Joshua Gee. ISBN# 0439922550
(Read selections.)
Or
Legends of Blood: The Vampire in History and Myth by Wayne Bartlett and Flavia Idriceanu. ISBN# 0275992926
(Read selections.)

Booktalk

Promote the book and read a selection from the text.

1. **Night Runner** by Max Turner. ISBN# 0312592280
   Zach must find out the solutions to many mysteries when he is broken out of a mental institution for a higher purpose.
2. **Suck it Up** By Brian Meehl. ISBN# 0385733003
   Morning wants to out vampires to the world, but there are many vampires who want to stop him.
3. **Thirsty** by M. T. Anderson. ISBN# 0763620149
   Should a new vampire join the community or be cured. Add that to real life drama, and the main character Chris has some decisions to make!
4. Vampire Island Series Adele Griffin
   Related to the fruit bat (not the blood sucking kind), these vampires siblings want to get rid of the non-vegetarian side.

Activity:
Blood!
Can you survive by drinking blood? Finding the answer to this can be a web search with an integrated searching lesson or it can be conducted via a pre-created Webquest with provided links such as:

http://wiki.answers.com/Q/How_much_blood_can_a_human_drink_before_getting_sick
http://answers.yahoo.com/question/index?qid=20090407131047AAjVuaZ
http://www.biology-online.org/biology-forum/about186.html
http://wiki.answers.com/Q/Is_it_healthy_to_drink_blood

Book Activity:
Vampire Bats: Hunting for Blood by Barbara A. Somervill. ISBN#1404238042
It's this or fleas!

Closing to Parents:
Thanks for coming today! I hope you learned a lot about the legends and the facts and found some great books to read!

Additional Activity Ideas:

Add werewolves and witches, and you have a full Halloween program.
Why are humans' teeth the way they are? What are we supposed to eat?
Learn about blood types.

This storytime was written by Stephanie G. Bauman.

Video Games

Anticipated Length: 1 Hour

Opening:

"**D**uring your time in the library today we are going to talk about gaming! Are you a gamer? Is it really rotting your brain? Not interested in games at all? Well listen up cause there is a lot of fun to be found."

Discussion:
Playing Games
Do you play games? How do your parents feel about it? Why do they feel that way? Solutions. If you don't play, why not? Is it too expensive? Aren't you interested in any games?

Book Activity:
The Ultimate History of Video Games: From Pong to Pokemon—The Story Behind the Craze That Touched Our Lives and Changed the World by Steven L. Kent. ISBN# 0761536434
(Read selections.)

Discussion:
Gaming Platforms: Computer, Nintendo, Xbox, Playstation, Handheld-Nintendo DS
Free online games, games days at library.
What about finding the right game for you?! (Games for girls, smarties, skill-hunting)

Activity:
Runescape
http://www.runescape.com/
This is a free online MMPO that is played through the browser, so nothing is downloaded.
If there are any concerns with content, try a free edutainment game:
http://medmyst.rice.edu/
http://www.amnh.org/nationalcenter/infection/03_inf/03a_inf.html
http://fas.org/immuneattack/

Discussion:
Can gaming be good for something besides entertainment?
Benefits: http://www.selfgrowth.com/articles/10_Benefits_Of_Video_Games.html
(This is not a scientific article, but is great for generating talk and ideas.)

Book Activity:
Careers in Gaming
Video Game Developer (Cool Careers) by Chris Jozefowicz. ISBN# 143392157X
(Read selections.)
You Can Be a Woman Video Game Producer by Judith Love Cohen and Nicole Willick.
ISBN# 1880599732
(Read selections.)

Closing to Parents:
Thanks for coming in today and learning more about video games. It can be a hobby, a talent, or even a future career. As a bonus playing them can even be free!

Additional Activity Ideas:

Guest speaker who works in the video game industry. (You would be surprised how many are around).

Conduct a game tournament even if you have to bring your gaming system from home.

Create a collection of free online edutainment games and show children how to access them.

Video Game art lesson

This storytime was written by Stephanie G. Bauman.

7

Series Programs

Having the same group of children at a repeating interval offers the exciting opportunity for a series storytime program. This may be as simple as reading a chapter book all the way through bit by bit. Or it can be as complex as a semester-long, curriculum-based, teacher-aided program. The idea is that this repeated amount of time offers the ability to build or expand a central theme. Learning about *urban gardening* or the *cultures of the Native Americans* does not have to be squeezed in to 45 minutes and can now become an amazing opportunity for children to get into the library and really learn more about and gain experience about a subject. Having a repeated time with the same students is an opportunity that should not be missed. The following Series of Programs offer some ideas of what is involved, and a scope of what is possible. Dare to dream big! Apply for grants, be creative, the sky is not the limit! You may find that the outcomes will be incredible.

Program #1

Theme: Your Past, Present, and Future
Audience: 6th Grade Students (ages 11–12)
Timing: 8 (2-hour) meetings + 1 optional presentation session
Program created by Stephanie G. Bauman
Resources necessary: computer access, chalkboard or whiteboard.
Resources beneficial: scanner, digital camera, guest speakers, suggested books,
   color printer.

Introduction:
Multiple literacy skills are the primary focus of this program. Students will select, evaluate, cite, and use information sources to create projects from in-house materials as well as online digital sources and Web 2.0 programs. The students will need to use critical thinking and comprehension skills to develop the new understandings neces-sary to condense the information gathered into creating the writing portions in this program. Technology will be taught as a tool, not only for finding information but as a tool for learning. The children will be encouraged to learn and share with others, as they explore resources together, and present their capstone project to the group. This program will help the students begin the process of relating to the world from a broader perspective, while teaching them to use technology skills to make inferences and create real-world connections.
Given adequate funding, students will be given a hardbound printout of their final creations.

(A grant or donation is recommended for this portion. I recommend soliciting this from a locally owned copy shop.)

This program plan was created with the following standard in mind:
AASL's Standards for the 21st-Century Learner, 2007. Available at http://www.ala.org/ ala/mgrps/divs/aasl/guidelinesandstandards/learningstandards/standards.cfm.

Section 1—Your Past

Lesson 1—Genealogy Discussion

Additional Materials Needed: Handout of a family tree to take home; suggested books.

Discussion:
Today is the first lesson in a series for you to learn all about yourself! We will be learning more about your past, present, and future and then sharing it with everyone in an online project.

Today we are discussing your past! Not where you were born and grew up, but where your ancestors were born and grew up. The United States is known as a melting pot. Can anyone tell me why? That's right, almost everyone who lives here now, except Native Americans, had past relatives who moved here from another country. This is called immigration. This is a hot topic in the news today, since there are still many immigrants coming to the United States, and many who live here illegally.

When this country had more room left in it, moving to the United States was much easier. Often land was given away free as bribes to entice people to move here. We are going to be finding out where your relatives are from and why it is so important to know more about them. Even if your parents are not your birth parents, knowing about the past of your current family members can be fun and interesting.

Book Activity:
The Great Ancestor Hunt by Lila Perl Yerkow. ISBN# 0395547903
An inspirational book for children on why our past history is important. (Read selections.)

Discussion:
You have many reasons why it is important to know about your ancestors. Can anyone think of any? (List on board and discuss. Examples to discuss include medical-genetic, historical-learn about the past, interesting-learn about you.) Does anyone know about where their own ancestors came from? (Discussion involves student feedback.)

We are about to find out a lot more! We are going to look up our last names on the web and find out about them. If you were born in this country, your last name is usually your father's last name. That is a tradition in many countries. Nowadays, many women are choosing to keep their last names when they get married. They might like their maiden name rather than their husband's, they might already have a career established using their current name, and sometimes the man chooses to take the woman's last name. It makes no difference whether your mother kept her maiden name or took your father's name, finding out about both of your parent's backgrounds is necessary as it completes the picture of you!

Activity:
Webquest on Last Names

1. Read: About the origin and meanings of last names:
   http://www.mayrand.org/meaning-e.htm
2. Search for your last name meaning and country of origin.
   Record results in a word document, including any family crest and all citations necessary.
   http://surnames.behindthename.com/
   http://www.last-names.net/
   http://www.surnamedb.com/
   http://www.winslowtree.com/surname-meaning.php

3. Interesting Extras

    See how your last name/s is currently distributed in the United States!
    http://www.dynastree.com/maps

Homework Activity:

A family tree template is passed out. Students are instructed to fill out as much information as they can from family members at home, including their birth dates and both birth and death dates of their parents, grandparents, and great grandparents, and any fun stories they might remember. If any students feel this assignment may be difficult for a variety of reasons (e.g., the child lives in a single parent home and doesn't know anything about the other parent), they should be allowed to contact you for other persons to research.

Lesson 2—Family Trees

Additional Materials Needed: Family tree "homework" filled out.

Discussion:

Let's talk about what we were able to find out about our families. (Lengthy discussion about what the students found out) You can discuss their personal family tree as an example. Even if your parents were not able to help you much, we can try to find out more.

Book Activity:

Gwyneth's Secret Grandpa by Annie Morris Williams. ISBN#0964527278
(Read selections.)
A book about family discovery.

Activity:

Research on Your Family Tree

1. We are all going to create free accounts together for an ancestry Web site. It is a free 14 day trial. Then we will go through the steps together to find more ancestors.
    http://www.ancestry.com/
2. Record your results from home and from the ancestry search into an online family tree using one of the programs listed below.
    http://www.ancestry.com/ or http://www.familyecho.com/#edit:START

Discussion:

Were you able to find out anything? (Discussion about search results.) You can access and keep searching from home or on library pass time if you want more information. We also have books on the process if you want to check them out.

Homework Activity:

Bring a few older family photos, they will be scanned in for our final project.

Lesson 3—Country of Origin

Additional Materials Needed: Family photos from home, suggested book.

Discussion:

So far, we have looked at our own family's trees. Now we are going to spend some time looking at our country of origin. I know that many of you are a combination of ancestors from many countries. Today each of you will need to pick one relative and learn more about not only that country and the time period that your relative lived there, and we will be making "informed guesses" about why they would want to leave and immigrate to the United States.

Book Activity:

One Tiny Twig by Dan Rhema. ISBN# 0972983503

A great story about one child's search for their family tree and how it affected their life.

Activity:

Country of Origin Report and Exploration

1. Choose a relative who was born in another country, and for whom you know that person's birth year. Using the resources in this library, and online, find out more about that country and what was happening during the time period that your relative was living there. (Also collect images.)

    Record your results. It should include name of your ancestor, country of his/her birth, the year or time frame they lived in that country, and information about what was happening there during that time period. You will make a guess as to why your ancestor or their parents may have chosen to leave their home country and immigrated to the United States. Was there a war, famine, or do you think that they were just adventurous and wanted a change? Finish up with a description of what that country is like today and what your life might be like now if they had not left and you had been born there. (Remember to cite sources.)

2. Online resources that might help:

    http://www.scopesys.com/anyday/

    Learn what happened on any day in history with this online tool.

    https://www.cia.gov/library/publications/the-world-factbook/

    The *CIA World Factbook* has useful information about countries, including maps and flags.

    http://www.state.gov/r/pa/ei/bgn/

    U.S. Department of State background notes. You can access information on individual countries.

    http://www.cp-pc.ca/

    Cultural Profiles Project provides overviews of life in various countries.

    http://countryscorecard.com/index.htm

    Country Scorecard offers country statistics.

    http://www.atlapedia.com/online/country_index.htm

Altapedia Online contains full color maps as well as key facts and statistics on countries of the world.

http://kids.yahoo.com/

Find pictures, maps, issues, and sites for a variety of countries.

Discussion:

Did you find out a reason why you think your relative might have left? (Discussion about what students found out.) What would make you want to move out of this country? Would it be hard to learn another language? To fit in?

Homework Activity:

Bring in photos of your life, does not have to be you, for scanning, one from each year if possible, and one each from some special events, such as big trips or celebrations. These should be an image that represents that time for you.

Section 2—Your Present

Lesson 4—Personal Timeline

Additional Materials Needed: Photos of students lives, from home.

Discussion:

We have been learning about the history of your ancestors, which is a large part of your personal history. We are now going to be talking about your history. You have each been alive for over 10 years, which is called a decade! We are going to take a look at your own life and important events in your life so far. There is a saying that you can't know where you are going unless you know where you have been, so for the next couple of lessons we are going to be taking a much closer look at where you have been. You might have had lots of changes in your life, or very little. What happens to you as a child can affect what you do for the rest of your life!

Book Activity:

Boy: Tales of Childhood by Roald Dahl. ISBN# 0141303050
(Read selections.)

Activity:

Create a Timeline of Your Life

1. Using the program http://www.ourstory.com/ each of you will create a timeline of your life with pictures. Include important events in your own life, like your birth, moves, trips, siblings births, and fun days. Then look at a calendar to find guesses for any dates you are unclear on. Also include find important or interesting events that happened during your lifetime, especially if they have to do with you! (Like the XBox 360 system creation or the election of the first African-American president.)

2. Online resources that might help:
   http://www.slco.lib.ut.us/kidhistday.htm

Day you were born: facts and information about events that happened on that day
http://www.scopesys.com/anyday/
Learn what happened on any day in history with this online tool.

Discussion:

Did looking at your life in detail bring up anything? Did you draw a lot when you were little and still like to draw now? Did you move from the South and still like the food that is popular there? Did you go on a big trip and see a neat zoo, and want to work with animals someday? Sometime breaking up your life into chunks can remind you of a bunch of little stories of the events that you have lived through. Sometimes, especially looking back from my age, it's not the big moments that affect your life, but the little ones in-between that are the most special. Think of some interesting things that have happened to you or unique things about your family for the next lesson.

Homework Activity:

Bring a photo of yourself, unless you brought a current one today, or we will take one for you! Ask your parent(s) for a couple of fun stories about you that happened before your first memory.

Lesson 5—Autobiography

Additional Materials Needed: Possibly a digital camera, photos of students from home, suggested book.

Discussion:

Today we are going to take a closer look at our own lives. We have already been over the major events and created a fun timeline. Now we are going to create an autobiography. Does anyone know the difference between a biography and an autobiography? Is one more accurate? Why?

Book Activity:

How to Write Your Life Story by Ralph Fletcher. ISBN#0060507691
(Read selections.)

Activity:

Write a Short Autobiography and Create a Cover Image
Write your own autobiography! Minimum 1 page.
Suggestions:

> Paragraph 1: Introduce yourself. Provide details: birth date, location, family.
> Paragraph 2: Relate a story about yourself as a baby.
> Paragraph 3: Relate a story about yourself as a 2–5 year old.
> Paragraph 4: Relate a story or two about yourself from ages 5 to 10
> Paragraph 5: Tell a story about yourself now. What grade you are in, what are your favorite things to do are, and something funny that happened recently.

Photo of you:

> Scan in student photo or have the librarian take one.
>
> Create a fun cover page for your final project using: http://www.befunky.com/
>
> Create a representation of yourself that fits the image of who you are now. Are you fun and light and flowery? Are you dark and mysterious? The image of you needs to be recognizable.

Discussion:

Were you able to think of some fun stories? Does it give an accurate picture of your life? Were you tempted to gloss things over, or leave out the part where your grandma died, because it was too sad? When you read someone's biography or autobiography in the future, these are things to think about?

Homework Activity:

Next week we are going to talk about the environment, so think about an issue that affects you and the planet too that might catch your interest. Does your family keep the lights on all the time? Do you have a vegetable garden? Does your neighbor have solar panels?

Lesson 6—Your Environment

Additional Materials Needed: Suggested book

Discussion:

Today we are going to be talking about where we live now. I am an environmentalist. That is someone who cares about the planet and where it is going, who takes the time to get involved with its care on a global and personal level. Many issues in the environment are concerns. It's definitely not too late to fix things. Last time I asked you to think about an issue that has caught your attention. Let's talk about some of these. (Discussion here.)

Book Activity:

Mission: Planet Earth: Our World and Its Climate—and How Humans Are Changing Them by Sally Ride and Tam O'Shaughnessy. ISBN#1596433108
(Read selections.)

Activity:

Your Environment and How to Help It

1. Choose an environmental issue and create a half page summation of the issue, also download one picture.
2. Find or think of ways that you and your family can help with this issue. Think global and local. Create a half page summation of these solutions, and download one picture.

3. Online resources that might help:

> http://www.webdirectory.com/ Amazing Environmental Organization Web Directory. The Earth's biggest environment search engine. Search for information on pollution, recycling, animal rights, wildlife and more!
>
> http://www.globe.gov/ Explore the Globe Program. Environmental issues, concerns, and solutions.

Discussion:

Let's go around the room and share the issue we looked at and give one solution that the other students can do to help that issue. Is there an environmental issue that concerns you that you don't think you can help with? Like whale hunting? You can help in a number of ways! (Discussion of ideas like fundraising, donation of money, helping save animals on a local level or volunteering.) They say the best way is to start locally and then think globally. Here are some other issues that we can talk about that aren't being mentioned by your reports. (examples: home gardening, bicycling, rainwater storage.)

Homework Activity:

Next time, we will be talking about who you want to be, both as a person and for a career.

Section 3—Your Future

Lesson 7—Future Exploration

Additional Materials Needed: Guest Speakers

Discussion:

"How many cares one loses when one decides not to be something but to be someone." Coco Chanel, Clothing Designer and more!

Everyone is always asking you what you want to be when you grow up, about your future career, but what about the future you? What kind of person do you want to be? After all you are more than just your career. You can be a nice actor who is fun, intelligent and the life of the party, or you can be a cranky mean spiteful actor who is snobby and only has fake friends. The career you want will be there for you, but what kind of person do you want to become?

Guest Speakers: (One that is fun and exciting and one that "seems" practical.) Examples: Computer Programmer (20 minutes) and Local Artist (20 minutes)

Activity:

Report on the Future You!

1. Choose a career that you would like to do and find out more about it, using resources in this library, and on the web. Something to think about: What will get you this career? Luck, Skill, Talent, Education?

Using any resources, create a half page document about what you would like to be for a career and what it will take to get it. Find and save an image of the career you are writing your report.

2. Online resources that might help:
> http://www.kids.gov/6_8/6_8_careers.shtml
> http://www.careervoyages.gov/students-elementary.cfm
> http://www.careerkids.com/careers/
> http://www.khake.com/page64.html

3. Think about what qualities a person is this field should have? Are these qualities you aspire to? For instance, a stockbroker on Wall Street has to have high energy, dedication, and will have little free time.

> Does this sound like something you want? What kind of _____ do you want to be? Do you want to be the kind of movie star that will hit journalists for taking your picture at the grocery store, or the kind that always has time for their fans? Finish your paper with what kind of _____ you would like to be.

> List personality and lifestyle traits that you think are needed for success. Describe what that would look like. Will you need to change your personality to be that person?

Homework Activity: If you forgot to bring pictures for any of the lessons, now is the time!

Lesson 8—Future Exploration

Discussion:
We have looked at where you come from, who you are, the world you live in, and who you want to be. Today we are going to put that all together and share it with everyone. We are going to make a Google presentation all about you! Together, we are going to open the program and learn how to start the process.

Activity:
Creating a Google Presentation (A Free and Easier Version of PowerPoint)

1. Create a Google docs account and choose to start a new presentation.

> Although many additional slides can be added for pictures from the web and from home, a basic final presentation should looks like this:
>> Cover page of student
>> Title page: student name, program name, year
>> Last name and meaning
>> Any last name pictures like a family crest
>> Family tree
>> Photo of ancestors
>> Country of origin (summary)
>> Pictures of country of origin

Personal timeline
Photos from timeline if not included on timeline
Autobiography
Your environment summary
Any pictures of environment from report
Your future report
Any pictures of future career or personality traits
Save the final document as both a PPT and PDF format

Lesson 9—Presentations

Project Presentations
Additional Material Needed: Projector and color printer access

Discussion:
When we meet people, we tend to make assumptions based on their appearance. If you see someone that is overweight, you might think that they are lazy and like to eat, but they could have a medical condition, or it could be a genetic pre-disposition. Learning more about where you came from, and who you are now, and the kind of person you would like to become one day is more than just about you. It is about looking through those first impressions and allowing a person to become more than just a snap judgment. Each of us is made up of a past and much of a present that is not of our choosing, but knowing about it and learning from it, is the first step in becoming your own person and the person you would like to be in your future.

Activity:
Presentation Sharing
Each of you will share your presentation with the class, just a sentence or two to sum up each slide.

Important Note:
As a capstone to this course, the Google presentation or the documents that made up this project, including photos, family trees, and assignments should be printed and bound per resources at hand or professionally done with hardback bindings (per a grant or donation).

Program #2

Theme: Community Helper Fair

Audience: 2nd–3rd Grade Students (ages 7–9)

Timing: A prep program that should be repeated for multiple groups and a final program

Based on the Program created by Ashley Sealey

Resources necessary for prep program: ball of yarn, photos of community, suggested book.

Resources necessary for final Program: Guest speakers from the community.

Introduction:

It is important for children to have a sense of belonging in their community. Recognizing that they are a part of a complex social group gives them a greater sense of identity. In addition, through learning about the various roles of members of the community, children are able to develop a greater understanding of careers. They will learn that every type of job plays an integral role in the community of which they are a part. Hopefully children will begin to connect the community helper's roles with their own skills, likes and dislikes. This will begin consideration of what avenues they might like to pursue in the future. It is my belief that a good age to begin planting these seeds of ideas in young minds is in grades 2 and 3 (ages 7–9). Public library youth librarians could work in partnerships with local school librarians on a project to increase awareness of community roles to these age groups.

In doing this, these collaborating librarians could conduct a Community Helper Fair. At this fair, children would be invited to get to know the police officers, librarians, doctors, shopkeepers, plumbers, and so on in their community. They would be encouraged to ask questions and have a look at some of the things that the helper's do on a daily basis. For example, a child might like to see how heavy a postal worker's bag is, or try using a doctor's stethoscope.

To prepare children for this exciting opportunity, the librarians would suggest that classes visit their school, and if a site visit could be arranged, to their public library for a 60-minute program about community helpers. It would be a good time to introduce the class to the collection and services at the public library. If the public library visit cannot be arranged, the children's librarian should be invited on that day for an outreach visit to the school. This program would introduce the concept and educate the children about how people work together to enrich a community. This would broaden the children's understanding and peak their interest about the topic. It would also allow them the opportunity to give some thought to who they might like to meet at the Community Helper's fair and what they would ask them.

Prep Program: (60 Minutes)

Opening:
Hello everyone. Welcome to the library (for both the school or public librarian; or, if doing an outreach visit . . . I am glad to visit your school today). Today I am really happy to be telling you about an exciting event that will be happening at the library next week. It is called the Community Helper's Fair.

Today we will be getting ready for the event together by talking all about the helper's in our community. First of all, does anyone know what a community is? (a group of people who interact together in a particular place.) Our community is where we live together. Our town/city is a community, our neighborhood is a community. What sorts of things do we find in our community? I'll give you a hint. (If children have come to the public library, "You have come to visit one of the places today?")

Activity:
Picture Your Community
(In preparation for this activity take some pictures around the neighborhood of local institutions, hangouts and/or landmarks. Be sure to include the public library and the children's school.)

Let's look at some pictures from our community together. If you recognize the place in the picture, put your hand up. If I call on you, see if you can tell me what the place is and whom you might find there. Would you find a trash collector on the street? A police officer?

Book Activity:
What is a Community? A to Z by Bobbie Kalman. ISBN#0865053847
(Read selections.)
This informative book looks at how communities are interdependent and reminds children that planet Earth is their most important community.

Activity:
Game: Web of Life—Community Helpers
This activity is intended as a way for the children to see the way that members of the community interact with and depend on each other to thrive. Prepare one piece of 8.5 by 11″ paper with each of the helper roles on one side, and their statements on the other. Here is a list of the helpers and their statements:

BABYSITTER:	A small fire starts while I'm watching my children. I call the **firefighter**.
FIREFIGHTER:	I rescued a hurt cat from a tree. I will call the **veterinarian**.
VETERINARIAN:	On my way to pick up my child at school I waved at the **crossing guard**.
CROSSING GUARD:	I am feeling ill, I will call the **doctor**.

DOCTOR:	Please take this prescription to your **pharmacist**.
PHARMACIST:	This ad in the newspaper says they have a new **chef** at my favorite restaurant.
CHEF:	I am going to make something tasty, with vegetables grown by the **farmer**.
FARMER:	I am waiting for the **letter carrier** to deliver my mail.
LETTER CARRIER:	I need to call the electrician to fix my refrigerator.
ELECTRICIAN:	I put wires in the new houses built by the **construction worker.**
CONSTRUCTION WORKER:	I buy materials to build houses from the **shop keeper.**
SHOP KEEPER:	My **bus driver** asked me to bring him an avocado on my way home.
BUS DRIVER:	I pick up the **hairdresser** after she has worked all day fixing hair.
HAIR DRESSER:	All of the sinks are jammed up with yucky hair, I call the **plumber**.
PLUMBER:	You will need to give these seeds that are clogging your garbage disposal to the **garbage collector.**
GARBAGE COLLECTOR:	I fell at work and chipped my tooth. I call the **dentist**.
DENTIST:	I fill a cavity for the **student** who ate too much candy.
STUDENT:	Our **building engineer** stopped picking up trash long enough to help us plant flowers in front of the school.
BUILDING ENGINEER:	I have an appointment today to talk to a **banker** about my loan for a new house.
BANKER:	When you take the **baby sitter** home this afternoon, remember to ask her if she is available next Saturday evening.
ADD YOUR OWN	(based on roles in your local community).

Children are each is given one piece of paper and assigned a job. Each child must create a statement that shows how that job relates to another student's job as suggested in the above list. If the children are very young, they may be assigned a partner to work together. Children can get really creative if they are allowed to choose their own community helpers. At the end of this exercise, each list can be read aloud.

Note: This program can also be divided into a weekly Community Helpers series. The prep program could start the series, followed by a series of themed weeks according to the guest speakers who will be present. Books, games and discussion would be customized to match the guest speaker. This could be anything from Hospital workers to Pet caretakers. See the storytime earlier in this book under 5–6 year olds called *Fire Safety and Awareness* for a great example.

Program #3

Theme: Our Planet

Audience: Elementary School Aged Children (ages 7–12)

Timing: Weekly

Based on a Program created by Kathy Burgener

Resources necessary: In-house book collection, guest speakers.

Resources beneficial: Internet, capacity for showing a movie, games, and prizes.

Introduction:

This program plan is to help familiarize students in a fun and interesting way with some of the science terminology they will be using in their classes. It is not intended to support any one year of schooling, but to be a general interest program giving them a little confidence with what they may be learning in school. This program will use items already owned by a city or county library system, such as books and videos or DVDs.

Invite as many speakers from the area who are willing to come for a short (free) lecture.

When this program is conducted in the public library there may be more room for fun because you won't need to tie it to a science curriculum making it free from the constraints of having to pack in terminology and conduct testing of the results. On the other hand, if this is tied to a part of the school's curriculum for that grade level, the students may benefit from follow-up sessions to help them retain what they have learned and apply their learning into their next project. Some suggested topics include:

1. Earth history: how the planet came into being including folktales from other cultures
2. Our sun
3. Our place in the universe and a little about the other planets in our solar system
4. Our moon and the view of our planet from it and space exploration
5. The Earth's oceans, seas, reefs, and sand
6. Drinking water and how our sewer system works
7. Mapping the earth and oceans
8. Forests, rainforests, woodlands—trees and plants
9. Carbon calculator
10. Weather
11. Earthquakes
12. Renewable energy
13. Recycling
14. Green Living

Groups to be approached for free speakers include The Nature Conservancy, local, state, or national park, a local wildlife refuge, a natural history professor with a biology background, a professor or graduate student from the Geography Department at local college, a representative from the local water district, a representative from power or gas company, and a representative from a renewable energy source.

Materials from the school library collection should be placed in an available location for the students to make choices. A collection of actual books and other resources from the city or county collection (or a bibliography or available resources) should be available for children to check out from the public library for further exploration on their own about the subject that was discussed.

 Notes

Program #4

Theme: Get Anime-ted!

Audience: Older Elementary School Aged Children (ages 8–12)

Timing: 5 meetings

Based on the program created by Melissa Castagna

Resources necessary: In-house book collection, one anime movie, paper art pens, and an anime bookmark. Other supplies include sticker print-outs from internet, glitter, and glue.

Resources beneficial: Contest prizes (unless you have a bunch of free promotion stuff around).

Introduction:

This program is a five week program for children ages five to twelve years old, to introduce them to anime, graphic novels, manga, and comic books written for their age level. This program will introduce a diverse range of reading materials such as wordless books and prose rewritten in comic book style, appreciation of different artistic styles, and will serve as a model for reaching out to the more reluctant readers.

Many children, especially boys, struggle with finding reading materials they really enjoy and that make them want to keep coming back for more. These new generations of children have been born in a world of technology and fast communication. They are surrounded, even immersed in technology and are accustomed to more visual and interactive experiences. Graphic novels, anime, and manga are a form of literature which fits this style of being highly visual, and the pictures and text are quite interactive. This form of literature has more recently been introduced in the United States and is especially new as a reading resource for younger children. Even the stories of Indiana Jones and Disney stories are being written in this format because people are recognizing how far-reaching the affects of this type of literature go. This new form of literature is also a way for parents and children to connect and understand each other. Parents and grandparents of this new generation will remember comic books and will be able to share this experience with their children and grandchildren.

Week 1:

The History of Anime, Manga, Comic Books, and Graphic Novels

We will display several examples of the artwork, talk about how anime/manga is read in a different way than other books the children have read and even how they are similar and different from our comic books. At this time we will introduce the Manga/ Fan fiction contest where everyone is invited to either write their own graphic novel/ anime short story or make their own anime/manga/graphic novel style drawing over the course of the program. They will be submitted during the fourth week for judging and we will have a showcase/award ceremony the fifth week.

Week 2:
How to Draw in Anime Style
Each child will be able to make their own anime drawing from a story of their choosing. Paper and art pens will be needed.

Week 3:
Anime Movie
The show must be geared toward the youngest group member. Alterations can be made by allowing older children to have discussion on art forms, story concept and suggested improvements.

Week 4:
Book Club Style Program
Everyone can talk about one graphic novel they have read and what they liked about it. If there is a lack of those who want to speak, the librarian can conduct a book talk to promote in-house collection. At the end of the discussion, the children will be able to make bookmarks using construction paper, anime images printed off the internet, stickers, markers, and so on. A guest speaker, such as a fan or comic book store owner, would be a great addition.

Week 5:
Anime Party
The fifth week will be the drawing/fan fiction showcase where we will display everyone's work and award the top three fan fiction submissions and top three drawings. Suggested prizes: graphic novel book, a "How to draw anime" book, stickers, or comic books. Children can also dress up as their favorite anime or comic book character. Play music and have fun!

Program #5

Theme: Disease
Audience: Grades 4–6 (ages 9–12)
Timing: Three 2-hour lessons (Can be subdivided based on time allocations)
Program created by: Stephanie G. Bauman and Lisa Katz
Resources necessary: Computer access, smartboard or chalkboard, books, movie.
Resources beneficial: Video camera, editing software, various materials required for Germ activities.

Note: Geared primarily for a school library, preferably to be co-taught by the teacher, it can be altered to work for a public library, especially an after-school program.

This program plan was created with the following standard in mind:
AASL's Standards for the 21st-Century Learner, 2007. Available at http://www.ala.org/ala/mgrps/divs/aasl/guidelinesandstandards/learningstandards/standards.cfm.

Introduction:
This program integrates science curriculum with twenty-first century literacy skills into a dynamic learning experience. The activities are accomplished through group work, individual activity, the exploration and use of multiple information types, technology use, and fun!

Lesson 1—What Is Disease?

Book Activity:
Fever 1793 by Laurie Halse Anderson. ISBN# 0689848919
(Read selections.)
This is a historical fiction book about the yellow fever epidemic in Philadelphia, which includes graphic detail and a mystery. People of the era did not know what caused the disease and neither do the readers.

Activity:
Catch a Disease!
Children choose a disease from a selection provided (or from a hat). They will work with this topic for the remainder of the program. This can be customized based on in-house resources.
(Examples include pneumonia, tuberculosis whooping cough, diabetes, anthrax, black plague, yellow fever, polio, cholera, chicken pox, lyme, leprosy, or measles.)

Tell the students they will need to look for information, and they will need to find out if they will live or not if they were to get one of the diseases!

Video Activity:

PBS Home Video: American Experience—Influenza 1918 (2005)
How scientists recently dug into the frozen tundra seeking DNA from that pathogen. Group discussion on what we know that they didn't in 1918?

Literacy Lesson:

How to Work in a Group
The teacher-librarian will give a short lesson/activity on group work strategies, including typical roles.

Activity:

Group Research Part 1

1. Students split into four groups and each group is assigned one pathogen (bacteria, viruses, fungi, protozoa).
2. Each group researches with information found in the library about the characteristics of this pathogen and how it spreads. They will need to be ready information and images. Suggested resources can include:

> http://kidshealth.org/kid/talk/qa/germs.html
> http://www.amnh.org/nationalcenter/infection/
> http://www.cdc.gov/ncidod/diseases/index.htm
> http://www.npr.org/templates/story/story.php?storyId=114075029

3. As a class they will come back together and create a smartboard chart for reflection. A printout will be given to each student.

Project Activities:

Individual:

Blog Part 1:

1. Students use library resources to find out more about what disease they have. They individually gather information on the disease they have. (Cause and symptoms.)
2. Integrated lesson on how to start a Blog and make postings.
3. Students will then create and post their own Blog postings on their disease. They will report journal style as if they really have the disease. They should include the disease, the symptoms, what they are going through, and what they have to live for. They can include photos.

Group:

Movie Part 1:

1. As a group students will decide on a theme for their movie on disease. Will it be a detective mystery? Will it be a CSI medical study? Will everyone in the school get sick? Will it be a disaster movie (a deadly truckload of pathogens fell over on the

freeway). The preliminary scenes are scripted and filmed. These scenes should pertain to the symptoms and types of pathogens and diseases.

2. Integrated lesson on movie creation: the use of the camera, how to download and save footage. plot development and writing, scenery and costume design, and choosing roles.

Additional Activity Ideas:

Students meet someone who has Lyme disease.

Students follow the blog online of someone who has an illness.

Students then write about a time when they were sick. What would they have shared in common with the blogger, what was different.

Students create a mini-documentary of a sick relative

Students have a Petri dish activity of their salvia culture.

Lesson 2—Prevention

How can we take care of our bodies so that we don't get sick?

Discussion:
Students talk about how not to get sick? What do they already know?

Reading Activity:
Students will choose a book or magazine related to disease from the library and be asked to skim it and read interesting sections during an allocated time slot. Students will give a short talk on their chosen item to the class. This will help everyone find resources for their disease.

Activities:
Germ Spreading (Choose one or more of the following options)

1. Bathroom Count: students fan out across the building to lurk all day in the bathrooms, counting the number of students who walk out without washing their hands. Keep count of these results.
2. Sparkles: one student who will pour sparkles on his/her hand. Then this student will shake hands with other students in the class. This activity will show the students how quickly germs can spread when hands aren't washed in the bathroom.
3. Hand washing Activity: students will have solution called Glogerm (or alternative) put onto their hands. Available from: www.glogerm.com. They wash their hands as normal. Then a black light is turned on, and they can see how many germs are actually left!
4. Fizzies Virus (KidZone http://www.kidzone.ws/plans/view.asp?i = 100). This is a mystery simulation activity on how disease spreads. Who has the new Virus?

   Some science type materials are required such as hydrogen peroxide and bleach.

Literacy Lesson:
More on Group Work
The class will discuss what worked and didn't work for them in their groups. Added suggestions for conflict resolution, communication and constructive criticism will be taught based on feedback.

Activity:
Group Research Part 2

1. The students will be re-grouped from the last unit's groups and again assigned a pathogen (bacteria, viruses, fungi, and protozoa).
2. They will explore how to *prevent* that pathogen (e.g., handwashing and clean water) as well as the diseases caused by the pathogen.
3. As a class, they will come back together and create a smartboard chart for reflection. A printout will be given to each student.

Project Activities:

Individual:
Blog Part 2

1. Students use the library resources to find out more about what disease they have. They individually gather information on the disease they "have" (Prevention methods).
2. Integrated lesson on Blogging safety.
3. Students create and post their own Blog postings on their disease. They will report journal style as if they really have the disease. For this lesson they will report on prevention. (Only if I had ... washed my hands or avoided a tick, or ...) They can include photos and other visuals.

Group:
Movie Part 2:

1. As a group students will create, script their plot, and act out new scenes pertaining to prevention.
2. Integrated lesson on Movie Creation: the use of the video editing program, inclusion of music and sound effects, writing, and filming techniques.

Additional Activity Ideas:

Students find out if they have a genetic history of disease from parents.
Students talk about diseases that they fear.
Students think of ideas for what to do if hand washing facilities are unavailable.
Make a 3-D clay model of an antibody and how it resembles a key that fits a microbe as a lock.

Make a funny comic strip containing at least five scenes how a character gets sick with a communicable disease. Make sure you include how they got sick and what virus or bacteria infected them.

Lesson 3—Treatment

How do I treat my disease?

Activity:
Play Games
Students play free online games about the immune system and disease treatments.

> http://medmyst.rice.edu/
> http://www.amnh.org/nationalcenter/infection/03_inf/03a_inf.html
> http://fas.org/immuneattack/

Discussion:
Students talk about the methods they learned in the games and already knew. Based on knowledge gaps, a lesson on the immune system and caring for your body should be conducted. (Other disease specific treatments will come later.)

Activity:
The school is a Body
In this activity the school building or public library represents the human body. A group of children act as the germs, and another group represents the various defenders. They have to research what their job is and present it to the class before the "invasion." Then an invasion happens!

Clear with the principal and teachers. It is similar to a game of tag, and if the antibody catches the germ, they are out; but the germs can reproduce by rescuing the hostage germs. The antibodies can do the same. Maybe there could be a surprise medication introduced that fights on the side of the antibodies. Whichever side that has the most players left wins!

Video Activity:
PBS Video DVD Secrets of the Dead: Killer Flu 2004

Activity:
Guest Speaker
Any guest speaker who has dealt with disease would be great!
Examples: heart disease, diabetes, cancer survivor, even food allergies. Ask them to talk about treatment and coping to be included in their story.

Activity:
Group Research Part 3

1. Students will be re-grouped from the last unit's groups and again assigned a pathogen (bacteria, viruses, fungi, and protozoa).
2. They will explore how to *treat* that specific pathogen.
3. As a class they will come back together and create a smartboard chart for a compare and contrast discussion. A printout will be given to each student.

Project Activities:

Individual:
Blog Part 3

1. Students use library resources to find out more about what disease they have. (Treatment methods).
2. Integrated lesson on what makes great Blog postings will be conducted.
3. Students create and post their own Blog postings on their disease. They will report journal style as if they really have the disease. For this lesson they will report on treatment. (If there is no treatment, what will they do?) They can include photos in their reports.

Group:
Movie Part 2:

1. As a group, students will create, script, and act out new scenes to complete the movie.
   This new scenes should pertain to treatment in regards to their chosen plot. Are the victims in the movie saved? How does it end?
2. Integrated Lesson on Movie Creation: Final touches, editing, how to burn to DVD

Additional Activity Ideas:

Students can create their own disease causing bacteria or virus.

Students should speak to their own pediatrician about the different immunizations they have had and what more are needed.

Students can interview a physician on the importance of the immune systems.

Students will create a pamphlet that describes their disease, gives preventative measures, and discusses any health measures that are available.

Conclusion:
In addition to twenty-first technology skills this program meets the following goals. Students will

- discover indicators of disease, the pathogens that cause them, the symptoms, treatment, cure and prevention through discussion, exploration, projects, and sharing.

- understand the relevance of disease in their own life.
- use technology to both explore and find creative understandings on disease and pathogens.
- experience a variety of information sources/types about disease and integrate them into discussion and projects.
- gain experience in group dynamics.
- make relevant connections and created dynamic suggestions for the group movie.
- combine learning experiences, new technology and creativity for Blog postings.

 Notes

Program #6

Theme: Role Models
Audience: 4th grade age (ages 10)
Timing: 4 Meetings
Program created by Stephanie G. Bauman
Resources necessary: computer access, computer games, art supplies.
Resources beneficial: guest speaker.

Note: Geared primarily for a school library, preferably to be taught in collaboration with one or more teachers. It can be altered to work for a public library, especially an after-school program.

This program plan was created with the following standard in mind:
AASL's Standards for the 21st-Century Learner, 2007. Available at http://www.ala.org/ala/mgrps/divs/aasl/guidelinesandstandards/learningstandards/standards.cfm.

Introduction:
During this program students will ask themselves "Do I need a role model and can I be a role model myself too?" They will discover the answer to this through multiple literacy exploration accomplished through group work, individual activity, thoughtful discussion and writing, and of course, fun!

Preparation:
1. Sign-up:
    Teacher or teacher librarian should sign up for the free site:
    http://www.heroicstories.com/
    It is an email posting of one real life hero a day. Examples should be used in Unit 3.
2. Purchase PC Games:
    Storybook Weaver 2004 (can be used in many contexts)
    http://en.wikipedia.org/wiki/Storybook_Weaver
    Fisher-Price Rescue Heroes: Mission Select 2000 (Or any of the Rescue Heroes Series).

Lesson 1—Superheros

Discussion:
Group Brainstorm Session

(Use a smartboard and print out for students if possible).
Here are some suggested discussion starters:

> What characteristics/qualities do super heroes have? (Compare to Idol)
> Can someone try to be a superhero or does it just happen?
> Can anyone become a superhero?
> Does a super hero have to have a magic power?
> If a superhero has a super power is it that person's job to use it to help others?
> What do super heroes do?
> · What happens if you are a super hero? What is your life like?
> What about the hero flaw? (Superman, Achilles)
> Can heroes make mistakes?

Activity:
Find a Superhero

1. Find a superhero anywhere in the library collection, including computers.
2. Sharing reading for 20 minutes (students can talk and share with each other!).
3. Students will write on the smart board characteristics and qualities that make their superhero successful.

Booktalk:
Any in-house materials about superheros that were missed by the students, should have a short presentation here.

Activity:
Hero Self Picture
Create a hero picture of yourself.
Students can use:

> http://www.ugo.com/heromachine/reallife/
> http://www.ugo.com/channels/comics/heromachine/classic.asp
> http://marvel.com/create_your_own_superhero

or they can create one on their own design.

Lesson 2—Villains

Discussion:
Group Brainstorm Session
(Use a *smartboard* and print out for students, if possible).
Here are some suggested discussion starters:

> What is a villain in a fairytale, book, or movie? Are they the same in real life?

Why is a villain bad?
Can you undo being a hero by becoming a villain?
What happens to villains?
Can you be a hero to some while being a villain to others?
Do you have to have a superpower to be a villain?
Discussion of villains . . .
Captain Jack Sparrow
    Robin Hood
    911 terrorists
Flipside of Heros previously discussed, who to whom were they not a hero?
What about small time villains? What actions should not be emulated?
Ambiguous villains? (overdue library fines? bullies? Someone does something wrong but isn't caught?)

Booktalk:
Any in-house materials about villains should have a short presentation.

Activity:
Pick a villain from your favorite movie or book

1. **Online Portion**—Student will find via a clip of the villain from a movie, a passage from a book, a drawing or illustration found online, or a drawing created by the student.
2. **Written Portion**—Answer the following questions (using a computer if you can):
   What made them bad? Who were they bad to?
   Were they always bad?
   Were they a hero to anyone?
   Did they have any good qualities?
   If they had done good deeds, using their power, what would their world be like?
   Is there a point in the story in which they could change their mind and do something good? If so when and what should they have done?
   If they got what they wanted, what would that place have been like? (e.g., Lord of the Rings. There would be no life, no way to feed orcs, everything dead, then the Sauron would have died too.)
3. **Presentation Portion**—Students give a short 5-minute presentation in groups to each other using their written answers and their presentation item.

Lesson 3—Real Heroes

Discussion:
Group Brainstorm Session
(Use a *smartboard* and print out for students if possible.)
Here are some suggested discussion starters:

What characteristics/qualities do real life heroes have?
What is the difference between a superhero and a hero?
Can you try to be a hero or does it just happen?
Can anyone become a hero?
Does a great deed (like being the first to sail around the world) make for a hero?
What do real life heroes do?
How would you know that you are a hero?
Are there different types of heroes?
Large scale
Just to one person
Do real heroes have flaws?

Activity & Discussion:
Local Heroes

1. Read some postings from http://www.heroicstories.com/
2. As a group search a local news Web site for the word hero.
   (This must be teacher-librarian searched due to some links to inappropriate content.)
   Example: www.ksl.com
   Hero is used quite liberally (sports, etc.)
3. Discussion on findings.

Activity:
Speaker (if possible)
Have local role model/hero come to class for talk/discussion afterward.

Webquest:
Heroes in History
Students use a pre-made webquest or visit the following sites and read about heroes in history.
While they are reading they make a list of qualities inherent to these heroes.
Do they match the ones the class thought of? Add new ones to smartboard.

Queen Elizabeth Spanish Armada Victory
http://www.elizabethi.org/uk/armada/
The Heroes of the Underground Railroad
http://www.nationalgeographic.com/railroad/
Heroes of World War 2
http://www.worldwariihistory.info/Medal-of-Honor/
(Pick three or four to read)
Hudson River Plane Crash Captain
http://www.wsbtv.com/news/18489417/detail.html
911 Firefighters

http://www.pbs.org/wnet/heroes/
Others:
http://www.heroesofhistory.com/page2.html

Activity:
Gaming
Students play: Fisher-Price Rescue Heroes: Mission Select 2000

Acting Out a Hero
Students will get into groups, create, and act out a heroic action that they read about or played on game.

Lesson 4—You Can Be a Hero!

Discussion:
Group Brainstorm Session
(Use a *smartboard* and print out for students if possible).
Here are some suggested discussion starters:

Is anyone in your life a hero?
Do they have qualities that are hero like?
Why does it matter to become a better person, more like hero, more like someone you look up to?
Can children be heroes?
What are small ways you can be a hero?
What are the signs of your success? (Sometimes there are none!)
When in real life is it important to be role model yourself?
How can you overcome any of your hero flaw/villain qualities?

Activity:

1. Students look at the Web site. . . .
   http://www.kidsareheroes.com/lily.php
2. Students choose a young hero and make their choice known to teacher and class when they have made their decision.

Activity:
Impromptu
Students can either be writers or actors. The writers create small scenarios for the actors to be age similar real life heroes. (For example, a little brother comes home from school and says he hates it. The actor then has a chance to make a positive impact.)

Activity:
You're the Hero Now!

1. Report:

    Create a short report answering the following questions.

    1. What hero-like qualities do you possess?
    2. What other qualities do you need to improve?
    3. Who might you try to help?
    4. How will you help them with your abilities?
    5. What is one thing you can do right now to be this person's hero?
        Attach to the back of your Hero Picture created in Lesson 1.

2. Switch it up:

    Give heroes out randomly to students

    They review the hero they received

    They each share with the class their 2 favorite things about that hero and members of the class get two guesses as to who it is. *Additionally*: These could be displayed in the library or hallway display cases. As word goes around, and others students start guessing, the creator may find themselves taking on the persona through making greater attempts to emulate the admirable qualities of their ideal hero self.

Activity:
Short Story
Student use program: Storybook Weaver 2004
To create a short story about their superhero self, must include examples of how they can help on a small level. (Saying something nice to a classmate, or redo a time when they had a missed opportunity.)

Conclusion:
In addition to twenty-first technology skills this program meets the following goals:

- To bring the "hero" into a realistic, reachable and relevant place for the students through discussion, exploration, projects, and sharing.
- To have a realistic view of people, everyone, even heroes and villains who possess both good and bad qualities.
- To understand the qualities role models possess that can and should be emulated.
- To experience a variety of information sources about heroes and integrate them into group discussion and projects.

Suggestion: Each lesson could be incorporated into a group blog and integrated technology lessons.

Index

About the Editor and Contributors

Editor

STEPHANIE G. BAUMAN earned her master's degree in library and information science from San Jose State University, San Jose, CA. In addition to authoring many of these storytime programs, she also compiled, edited, and provided The Owl illustration for this book. Stephanie plans to pursue her PhD. She enjoys spending time with her husband, hiking with her dogs, martial arts, arts festivals, outdoor music, yoga, and of course reading.

Contributors

All contributors to this book, at time of writing, were graduate students at San Jose State University Master of Library Information Science Program.

ASHLEY SEALY currently works as a Senior Library Assistant at the Maryvale Branch of the Toronto Public Library. She thoroughly enjoys developing and delivering innovative, fun and educational programs for children of all ages.

ELIZABETH TURNER works as a Library Media Assistant for Anaheim City School District. She loves working with children and sharing her love of books with them.

JAKE SEXTON works at the Encinitas branch of the San Diego County Library. His main focuses are technology and teen services.

JOSH MITCHELL is a Youth Services Librarian at the Encinitas Branch of the San Diego County Library. He wishes to thank his wife Holly and two-year-old daughter Ayla for their boundless love and inspiration.

JULIE ANDREWS-JOTHAM is the CEO of the Hastings Highlands Public Library in Maynooth, Ontario. She enjoys creating programs that will engage and inspire young readers.

KATHY BURGENER enjoys planning and hosting weekly preschool storytimes including flannel boards, puppets, songs, stamps, and crafts as well as reading books. She currently works at the Casa de Oro Branch of the San Diego County Library.

LISA KATZ will finish her MLIS and LT in May 2010, after which she hopes to return back to the teaching world by way of the library in the near future. She is a mother of two children, ages 9 and 13.

MELISSA CASTAGNA has enjoyed working for several years with children with autism and hopes to soon bring those fun experiences with them to the library as a children's librarian. She loves bringing the adventures found in books to life for children.

07/2011